101 ROMANTIC
WEEKENDS IN EUROPE

SARAH WOODS

M

First published in 2009 by
New Holland Publishers (UK) Ltd
London • Cape Town • Sydney • Auckland
www.newhollandpublishers.com

Garfield House
86–88 Edgware Road
London W2 2EA
United Kingdom

80 McKenzie Street
Cape Town 8001
South Africa

Unit 1, 66 Gibbes Street
Chatswood, NSW 2067
Australia

218 Lake Road
Northcote
Auckland
New Zealand

ISBN 978 1 84773 416 7

Senior Editor: Nicola Jessop
Designer: Roland Codd
Cartography: Stephen Dew
Production: Marion Storz
Publisher: Ross Hilton
Publishing Director: Rosemary Wilkinson

Reproduction by Modern Age Repro
House Ltd, Hong Kong
Printed and bound by Times Offset
(M) Sdn Bnd, Malaysia

The author and publishers have made every effort
to ensure that all information given in this book is
accurate, but they cannot accept liability for any
resulting injury or loss or damage to either property
or person, whether direct or consequential and
howsoever arising.

PHOTOGRAPHY CREDITS

p9 © Hemis/Alamy; p10 © LOOK Die Bildagentur der Fotografen GmbH/Alamy; p12 © JLImages/Alamy; p14 © EFE/UPPA/Photoshot; p15 © dbimages/Alamy; p16 © Alan Copson City Pictures/Alamy; p17 © www.splendia.com; p18 © Jim Craigmyle/Corbis; p19 © Ben Ramos/Alamy; p20 © Alberto Paredes/Alamy; p21 © Paul Ashby/Fotolibra; p22 © ORDI CAMÍ/Alamy; p25 © parisauthentic.com; p26 © Pidjoe/iStock; p27 © caracterdesign/iStock; p28 © Sources de Candalie; p29 © Alex Segre/Alamy; p30 © Chateau Villandry; p31 © Alain Doire-Bourgogne Tourisme; p32 © www.ot-epernay.fr tourist office of Epernay and its Region; p33 © Doug Pearson/JAI/Corbis; p34 © Deb22/iStock; p35 © Thierry Prat/Sygma/Corbis; p36 © Jon Arnold Images Ltd/Alamy; p37 © Les Roulottes; p38 © rivapr.co.uk; p39 © www.orionbb.com; p41 © Atlantide Phototravel/Corbis; p43 © Botanica/Jupiter Images; p44 and 45 © www.orientexpressimages.com; p47 © millsrymer/iStock; p48 © Rob Howard/Corbis; p49 © Fernando Bengoechea/Beateworks/Corbis; p50 © David Lees/Corbis; p51 © Bruno Morandi/Robert Harding World Imagery/Corbis; p52 © Atlantide Phototravel/Corbis; p53 © Sicily Art Hotel; p55 © Virgin Limited Edition; p56 © Hotel Uto Kulm; p57 © Felder Images; p59 © Luxembourg Government www.eu2005.lu; p61 © World Pictures/Photoshot; p62 © Alan Copson/JAI/Corbis; p64 © Lynette Thomas/Photoshot; p65 © Holland Info Store; p67 © Robert Harding Picture Library Ltd/Alamy; p69 © pederk/iStock; p71 © photo BBT; p72 © Martyn Goddard/Corbis; p74 © Federal State of Bavaria; p78 © www.romantischestrasse; p75 © Gregor Schuster/zefa/Corbis; p76 © Atlantide Phototravel/Corbis; p77 © David Wall/Alamy; p80 © ANTO/Osterreich Werbung/Diejun; p81 © ANTO/Osterreich Werbung/Weinhaeupl; p82 © ANTO/Osterreich Werbung/wiesenhofer; p83 © Gavin Hellier/Robert Harding World; p85 © Peter Adams/JAI/Corbis; p87 © www.filharmonie-brno.cz; p89 © Westend 61 GmbH/Alamy; p91 © Arco Images GmbH/Alamy; p92 © Mauritius World Pictures/Photoshot; p93 © Gregory Wrona/Alamy; p94 © Andrzej Gorzkowski/Alamy; p96 © Franz-Marc Frei/Corbis; p98 © BlueMoon Stock/Alamy; p100 © F1online digitale Bildagentur GmbH/Alamy; p101 © Walter Lockwood/Corbis; p103 © Jon Arnold Images Ltd/Alamy; p105 © Grand Hotel Europe, St Petersburg; p107 © Caro/Alamy; p110 © World Pictures/Photoshot; p112 © World Pictures/Photoshot; p115 © David Short Travel Photography; p116 © KAKU SUZUKI/amanaimages/Corbis; p119 © Bobo, www.slovenia.info; p121 © Macduff Everton/CORBIS; p122 © ANDREJ CRCEK/Alamy; p 124 © Nenad Banjac; p126 © Rod Edwards/Pictures Colour Library; p129 © Paul A. Souders/CORBIS; p130 © Picture Contact/Alamy; p131 © John Warburton-Lee Photography/Alamy; p132 © lee hacker/Alamy; p134 © Ritz Carlton; p135 © Jochen Tack/Alamy; p137 © John Warburton-Lee/John Warburton-Lee Photography, courtesy of Alison Wood, Grifco PR; p138 and 139 © The Rocco Forte Collection, www.thebalmoralhotel.com; p141 © www.uniquehomestays.com; p142 © www.thegoring.com; p143 © London Eye Image Library; p144 © www.bodysgallen.com; p146 © www.thespacompany. com; p147 © aloha_17/iStock; p149 © www.bluelagoon.com; p150 © Simon Lane/Alamy; p152 © credit Nancy Bundt/Innovation Norway; p153 © doescher /iStock; p155 © Blaine Harrington III/Alamy; p156 © credit Hakan Hjort; p157 © Jogan Furusjö/Alamy; p159 © www.kakslauttanen.fi; p158 © NordicImages/Alamy.

CONTENTS

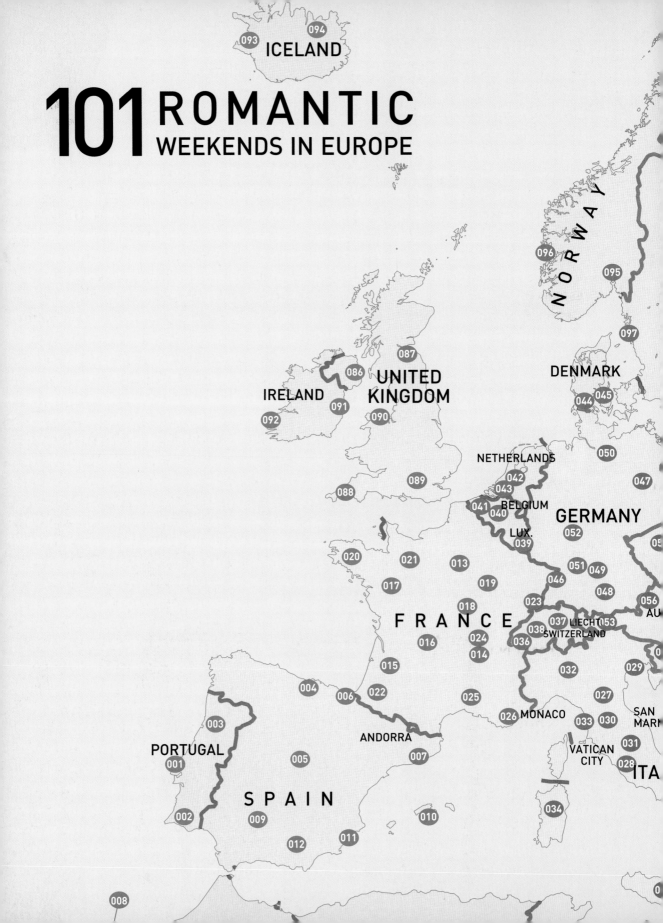

101 ROMANTIC
WEEKENDS IN EUROPE

PORTUGAL

TIME DIFFERENCE GMT +1

TELEPHONE CODE +351

CURRENCY Euro

LANGUAGE Portuguese

POPULATION 10 million

SIZE OF COUNTRY 88,889 sq km
(34,667 sq miles)

CAPITAL Lisbon

WHEN TO GO Mainland Portugal's winters are
exceptionally mild, especially in the Algarve region.
Cooler inland temperatures typify inland provinces,
with snowfall in the Serra da Estrela mountains.
Autumns are pleasantly warm, turning steadily
cooler into December. Islands offer year-round
temperate conditions – 18°C (64°F) in winter
and 22°C (72°F) in summer.

TOURIST INFORMATION
Portuguese National Tourist Office
Tel: 0845 355 1212
Fax: 020 7201 6633
Email: tourism@portugaloffice.org.uk
www.visitportugal.com

On the west of the Iberian Peninsula, Portugal's 830 km (515 mile)
Atlantic coastline flanks the nation to the south and west with the
Spanish border to the north and east. The River Tejo provides a neat
division across the country, stretching out to meet the waters of the
Atlantic in Lisbon. Portugal's 17 islands and atolls include the
archipelagos of Azores and Madeira. Many of Portugal's sleepy
fishing villages of brightly painted sardine boats, cobbled streets
and whitewashed houses sit alongside pristine beaches. Rugged,
windswept coastal enclaves evoke the nostalgia of Old Iberia and
are blessed with over 300 days of golden sunshine each year.

SINTRA

Sintra has long revelled in a reputation as an idyllic love-bird retreat, just a 40-minute drive from Lisbon and edged by beautiful, sheltered rocky coves. Stroll charming narrow streets, enjoy an enchanting journey through the town's historic centre in a horse-drawn carriage or picnic in the sweet-smelling gardens of Monserrate and the stunning park of Palácio da Pena. Described by Lord Byron as "Glorious Eden", Sintra's charms have been praised by writers ever since. Portugal's national poet, Luís Vaz de Camões, proclaimed Sintra's glory in his epic works *Os Lusíadas* (The Lusiads), drawing nobility and aristocrats to its historic architecture and lush flowers. Today, visitors keen to treat their loved ones like royalty should consider a romantic weekend in Sintra's handsome Tivoli Palácio de Seteais (Palace of the Seven Sighs), a distinguished late 18th-century castle built by the then Dutch Consul. If your idea of romance is to be joyously cocooned in cosseted luxury, then the Palacio de Seteais is your Shangri-la. Named in honour of a 12th century love story centred on an Arabian princess, the Tivoli Palácio de Seteais enjoys seductive seclusion in a quintessentially romantic niche amidst Gothic, Egyptian, Moorish and Renaissance art.

Expect opulent grandeur, tasteful dignity and every modern comfort in this perfect place for couples where romantic period elegance reigns. As befits its true neo-classical glamour, the Tivoli Palácio de Seteais is beautifully refined with lots of special touches for the romantic at heart. An impressive triumphal arch commemorates a royal visit while striking interiors are sumptuously appointed with fine antiques, tapestry, chandeliers and art. Marvel at fresco paintings, flowing drapes, polished woods, dazzling crystal, pewter, gilded motifs and towering floral displays. Lush, green gardens tumble down to a beautiful pool in a blissful romantic scene shielded by an exotic array of colourful pink and purple bougainvillea over garden trelliswork, red geraniums, eucalyptus, lemon trees and sweet mimosa. Choose from one of 30 rooms, each individually furnished in Baroque style with Champagne, heart-shaped pastries and hand-tied posies of romantic camellias on request.

HOW TO GET THERE
The Tivoli Palácio de Seteais is a 40-minute transfer from Lisbon by taxi or hire car

CONTACT
Tivoli Palácio de Setais
Tel: +351 219 233 200
Email: reservas.hps@tivolihotels.com
www.tivolihotels.com

The perfectly manicured grounds of the Palácio de Seteais, Sintra.

002

ALGARVE

HOW TO GET THERE
The resort is a 20 minute transfer from Faro International Airport by taxi or hire car

CONTACT
Royal Spa
Tel: +351 289 353 480
Fax: +351 289 353 476
Email: royalspa@vdl.pt
www.valedolobo.com

Since early times, fables and folktales have referenced salt in their fairytales. Salt has also been used in pottery production, was a source of medieval currency and, 4,700 years ago, was a pharmacological power. Salt has also played a vital role in religious ritual across many cultures, symbolizing immutable, incorruptible purity. There are more than 30 references to salt in the Bible, using expressions like "salt of the earth". A salt tax was a significant cause of the French Revolution; it also motivated American pioneers and is essential for the maintenance of human life. Since time immemorial, salt has been honoured for its health-giving properties and is used to treat asthma, eliminate toxins, boost metabolism, enhance circulation, soften skin and improve well-being – and more. Little wonder that the Algarve's prestigious Royal Spa pays homage to Portugal's 2,700-metre rock-salt caverns at Loulé. Formed by the geological separation of Europe and Africa before the Jurassic era, the salt vein stretches as far as Barcelona and is one of Europe's richest natural therapeutic salt sources.

Sitting within the Vale do Lobo resort, the Royal Spa applies 'healing through water' (Latin: *sanus per aquum*) from which the SPA acronym derives. Based on the principle that water is the very origin of life and possesses special healing powers, the sanctum of water is honoured in the prevailing influences of Vale do Lobo's environment: the Atlantic Ocean and the lagoon-system and dunes of the Natural Reserve of the Ria Formosa. From the sandy beaches of Ancão to the charming village of Cacela Velha, the natural inlets of the Ria Formosa offer wildlife-rich wetlands, peaceful waters and deserted isles. Gushing fountains, trickling waterfalls and stunning cascades are evident in the spa's design and play an important role in mind, body and soul therapies, from hydrotherapy showers and hydro-massage treatments to steam therapies – many using health-giving salt. Treatments focus on organic plant extracts, sea algae and natural essence oils. Generous use of stone, wood and plants throughout provide a mirror on the surrounding natural world.

The palatial Royal Spa may be ultramodern in construction but this 4,000 sq metre (43,000 sq ft) purpose-built wellness sanctuary draws inspiration from ancient health philosophies. Oriental and western techniques run side-by-side with traditional Chinese medicine complemented by aqua-therapies. Nutritional advice and minor cosmetic surgery are also available, in conjunction with Dr Thomas Kaiser, Director of the Vale do Lobo Medical Centre. The mood is mellow, the setting upmarket but not stuffy, and free from boot-camp deprivation. Physiological assessments help to identify individual health objectives using a holistic approach, from mud baths, hot stones, Reiki and ice therapies to weight loss and stress

management. Ten therapy suites each bear the names of flowers indigenous to the local area together with two wooden spa pavilions set in quiet Oriental-style gardens around a white pebble waterfall and lily pond. Choose from saunas, a Turkish bath and steam rooms infused with local essential oils. Gentle water jets sooth fatigued limbs while salt peels soften, and deep, iced curative pools rejuvenate. Age-old touch therapies rid stressed joints of gnarls and knots while muscles are eased and vitality is restored.

In keeping with the royal theme, the Royal Spa menu is fit for a king, with specially created dishes by Chef Maurice Belhaj in collaboration with British diet and fitness expert Rosemary Conley. A mouth-watering array of dishes centres on simple fresh local produce and organic salads and vegetables together with a menu of health-giving juice drinks using energy-boosting ingredients blended to help brighten skin, heighten mood and enhance libido. Choose a refreshing pineapple, mint and ginger melange for a tasty mid-morning pick-me-up to experience an uplifting zingy surge that lasts well into the afternoon.

Long, uninterrupted sleep is a common theme of folkloric culture in Portugal with myths centring on the therapeutic powers of local nuts, fruits and berries. In the Royal Spa, undisturbed restfulness is aided by soothing massages that help to nurture quality sleep. Gentle pressure applied to the head, neck, shoulders and spine can ease areas of tension that lead to the build-up of stress. Sweet-smelling blends of warmed essential oils induce a deep state of relaxation and calm with the Royal Spa's soothing thyme herbal tea infusion – the perfect aid to restful slumber.

From the moment you enter the Royal Spa, you can immerse yourself in a haven far from the stresses of daily life.

003 MADEIRA

CONTACTS
Madeira Botanical Gardens
Tel: + 351 291 211 200
Fax: + 351 291 211 206
Email: jardimbotanico.sra@
gov-madeira.pt
www.madeirabotanicalgarden.com

*The Madeira Botanical
Gardens are lush, vibrant
and breathtakingly beautiful.*

Madeira's treasured 80,000-sq metre (861,120 sq ft) botanical amphitheatre not only contains a dazzling array of over 2,500 plant species but also offers spectacular panoramic views across mountains, bay waters and the city below. Look out across glorious, ramshackle rooftops to dramatic peaks and the deep blue Atlantic from Madeira's cool leafy enclave where Japanese pagodas and romantic follies lie tucked amidst soaring ferns. Stroll along pebble-dotted pathways past ponds straddled by delicate wooden bridges. Discover handkerchief-sized plazas, boulder-strewn rockeries and crashing waterfall cascades fanned by giant creeper-clad palms. Or hike the orchid-rich leafy trails amongst a kaleidoscope of velvety pink and yellow blooms.

A romantic notion conjured up the Reid family in 1881, the Madeira Botanical Garden boasts a privileged location on the south side of a valley. At an altitude of between 200 and 350 metres (660–1,155 ft), conditions are perfect to support a spectacular array of exuberant vegetation. Nourished by nutrient-rich soils, the gardens are lush, vibrant and breathtakingly beautiful – just as the founders had dreamed. Revel in the fragrances of sprouting herbs, sub-tropical fruits and slender pine trees or discover semi-arid succulents and the dragon tree with its cylindrical trunk. A pattern of harmonious shapes and contrasting colours uses the vivid hues of Funchal Bay as a backdrop to create a tapestry-like floral carpet. Exotic plants from all continents combine to produce a glorious celebration of colour, from lilies, birds of paradise, magnolias and azaleas to bromeliads, cacti and hibiscuses.

For a truly romantic voyage through the gardens and beyond, take the Botanical Garden's cable car up to the historic village of Monte with its beautiful church, gardens and wicker sledges. Savour expansive vistas of stunning tropical splendour, romantic Oriental tea-gardens and secluded love-seats tucked amongst the palms. Gaze out across the Atlantic Ocean as you cosy up in silent wonderment to the gentle sounds of seabirds and lapping waves. Monte's fairytale aura once captivated Europe's high society; today it is synonymous with miracles and centuries-old romantic legends. Since 1850, couples have observed the tradition of sliding at high speed on two-seater toboggans along Monte's narrow, winding streets down to Funchal. Steered by two men dressed in traditional white cotton clothing and straw hats, the sledges glide on wooden runners. Poles are used for propulsion and rubber-soled boots as brakes, so lock hands and close your eyes for this romantic leap of faith.

SPAIN

Spain has at least a dozen personalities, from the desert-style plains of Almeria and silver-sand beaches of Formentera to the curvaceous hills of Catalonia and the deep ravines, stalagmites and caverns of the Balearics. Vast highland plateaus are segmented by spiny mountains while narrow, low-lying coastal plains run like ribbons throughout the south-west. Dramatic cliffs are home to hook-clawed raptors while bears, lynx, and wolves roam mountain woods and streams. Vines, olives, figs and orange groves flourish in the fertile soil of the foothills while beautiful domed Moorish palaces sit in resplendent gardens amidst mosaics, frescoes and archways.

TIME DIFFERENCE GMT +1

TELEPHONE CODE +34

CURRENCY Euro

LANGUAGE Spanish

POPULATION 40.4 million

SIZE OF COUNTRY 504,782 sq km (196,865 sq miles)

CAPITAL Madrid

WHEN TO GO Spain is generally divided into a temperate north and a hot, dry south, with April to October the most popular time to visit. In the height of summer (July to August) temperatures soar to scorching highs inland. Coastal regions remain pleasant year-round but are prone to wet weather in winter.

TOURIST INFORMATION
Spanish Tourist Office
Tel: 020 7317 2010
Fax : 020 73172 048
Email: londres@tourspain.es
www.tourspain.co.uk

004

SANTANDER

CONTACTS

Santander International
Music Festival
Tel: +34 942 210 508 / 942 314 853
Fax: +34 942 314 767
www.festivalsantander.com

Cuban dancer Lorna Feijoo, of the Boston Ballet, performs during a rehearsal of Les Sylphdes for the Santander International Festival.

August in Santander is set to a romantic musical score as breathtaking, rapturous symphonies and stirring concertos fill the city with wisps of harmonic joy. Moving orchestral drama evokes the passion of heart-rending tragedy while soulful sonatas and *concerto ritornelli* whirl through Santander like a melodic virtuosic cyclone. From sweet piano refrains and dancing violins to cello solos and full orchestral might, the city plays host to umpteen renditions and repertoires from every classical genre. Delight in moody *modernisti* movements and the delicate Romantic era's lyrical touch during Northern Spain's month-long celebration of music that culminates in a rousing performance by the National Orchestra of Spain.

Named for the Latin *Sancti Emeterii*, Santander is characterised by fine historic buildings on handsome, Roman-built streets lined with trees and shrubs. At the heart of the city, the garden-filled Paseo de Pereda boulevard splits the old quarter from Santander's sandy, coastal strip. One of the city's earliest constructions, a 13th-century cathedral, sits atop catacombs, underground sculpture and sombre, vaulted chambers close to the grand bourgeois mansion houses overlooking the Bay of Biscay. Here, the Palacio de Festivales (Festival Palace), built by Francisco Javier Sáenz de Oiza, is the venue of the prestigious Santander International Festival, one of Spain's oldest musical celebrations. Though smaller performances can be enjoyed in the intimate setting of over 40 historic cloisters and gardens across the city, it is the Festival Palace that embodies the spirit of the occasion from a full-on symphonic extravaganza that sets the tone of the many dozens of operatic and choral concerts that follow. Inaugurated in 1991 with Handel's oratorio, *Joshua*, a stirring piece from the height of his late creative period, the Festival Palace is in its element with big-stage productions mixing historic, ecclesiastic and aristocratic elements with a flavour of the mountains and the sea. The venue's haunting acoustics blend with a stunning stage set – a large window that frames the Bay of Biscay provides the backdrop. To the sound of rapturous applause, the scenery takes on a romantic fervour at the climax of the festival when showered with thousands of single-stem roses from the stalls.

CONTACT
Madrid Tourist Office
Tel: +34 915 881 636
Email: turismo@munimadrid.es
www.esmadrid.com

Dance a fiery salsa for a burst of sensual energy.

MADRID

Madrid's sultry salsa scene revels in sensual seduction, in which simmering physical chemistry and overtly sexual rhythms collide in a full-on sensory assault. Meaning 'sauce' in Spanish, the salsa is anything but sweet in style. Yet a fiery chilli has soft flesh and the salsa is no stranger to tender sentiment, albeit wrapped in raw, heartfelt desire. With bodies pressed tightly together in rhythmic unison, Madrid's spellbinding musical love potion adds an extra frisson to the dance-floor. 'I'm drowning and I can't live without you' resonates the ultimate salsa love cry of *Mi Todo* (My All): an intimate cocktail of intoxicating lyrics and irrepressible, sweat-drenched beats.

In recent years salsa musicians from such places as Havana, Panama, Colombia and Argentina have made their home in the Spanish capital, joining forces with Spanish musicians to create various hybrid forms of salsa fused with African and Middle Eastern sounds. In Madrid, this melting pot of vibrant musical influences is easy to discover, from Cuban folk and Puerto Rican peasant dances to the tribal drumming of the Western Sahara. Visitors keen to experience Madrid's sassiest dance form will need to wait until at least midnight when restaurants begin clearing the last dinner plates and city's salsatecos begin to fill. Entering a salsa bar can be like joining a theatrical production where the dance floor is the stage and the *salseros* the actors. To the 1-2-3-touch, 5-6-7-touch of a pulsating, syncopated beat a moving sea of dancers revels in physical, musical and philosophical synch. Through shifting moods and tempos, couples sustain an intense level of inter-body communication as tendrils of salsa passion ignite.

Pick up a *Guía del Ocio* from any street corner kiosk for a comprehensive list of salsa lessons, venues and festivals, plus upcoming events. Madrid's premier salsa joints include the trendy Barnon (17 Santa Engracia), tropical *Azúcar* (Pº Reina Cristina, 7, near Atocha Railway Station) and the fiesta-loving *El Son* (Victoria 6, Metro Sol, near Puerta del Sol). The city's oldest *salsateca, O'zona* (Av. Mediterráneo, 12 Metro Conde de Casal o Menéndez Pelayo), may boast a pocket-sized dance-floor, but for a shock of sensual energy few can compare. A blaze of fast-paced spins and turns ensure a night of tight-fit dances among the salsa throng. Once the triple-twirls fade into a dreamy, slow-tempo *salsa romántica*, you'll know daybreak has arrived.

006

CONTACT
Cantabria Tourist Department
Tel: +34 942 208 299
Fax: +34 942 208 286
www.turismodecantabria.com

Food is exaulted with near-religious fervour in San Sebastian.

SAN SEBASTIAN

Romance in Spain conjures up visions of delicious tapas and free-flowing sangria overlooking the sea. Sharing mouth-watering regional delicacies in a warm sea breeze epitomises the beguiling romantic mellowness of the Spanish coastline where exquisite seafood dining wows gastronomes from around the world, especially in San Sebastian in the north. Chefs throughout Spain speak of San Sebastian in gushing superlatives; this gastronomic stomping ground boasts extraordinary acclaim. Blessed by food-rich geography, San Sebastian (or *Donostia* in Basque) is the nation's gourmand capital: an epicurean epicentre that boasts the highest concentrations of Michelin stars on the planet. Gourmet dining is a way of life in San Sebastian where menus deserving of rapturous applause are tantamount to the city's daily bread. Stroll around San Sebastian's scallop-shaped bay to discover rich and sumptuous culinary genius, be it a cosy, family-run cafe or a seductive candle-lit bistro. Everyone is a connoisseur in this gastronomic heaven where food is exalted with near-religious fervour and wine consumed with devout zeal. Dubbed 'The Best Place to Eat on Earth', San Sebastian draws on some outstanding regional ingredients, from succulent sardines, squid and tuna to tangy sheep's-milk cheeses and juicy berries.

In centuries past, San Sebastian's quaint belle époque coastal location provided a fashionable summer getaway where the affluent elite could escape the overpowering heat of the city. Today, the city continues to attract a moneyed mix of haughty aristocracy and blue blood together with a legion of foodie pilgrims seeking the ultimate gourmet experience. On the basis of its unforgettable gastronomic heights, San Sebastian is synonymous with romantic proposals and amorous rendezvous where wine and food play a starring role. Fine 19th-century grandeur fans out from wide promenades to cobblestone streets and plazas perfectly framed by mountainous countryside and the crashing waves of the Atlantic Ocean. On the *Paseo de la Muelle*, fishing boats can be seen unloading their catch straight to the restaurants on the dock. For just-caught freshness, grab a rustic table on the harbour-side at lunchtime and ask to sample the latest haul cooked with olive oil and lemon. You don't need to locate a French accolade in order to dine like a king in San Sebastian. Pop open a bottle of citrus-rich, semi-sparkling Txakoli, San Sebastian's so-called 'romance in a glass' to witness show-offy waiters pour this light and fragrant white wine from great heights to give it extra fizz.

BARCELONA

Sharing a few intimate moments of peaceful 'togetherness' amidst Barcelona's urban melee requires calculated planning. Noise permeates every stratum in a glorious metropolitan chorus of roaring traffic and blaring horns. Seductive and inviting, Barcelona's buzzing vibe lures you in before delivering a mind-blowing sensory assault. Streetwise and stylish, it mixes contemporary architecture with wild imagination, adding tradition, style, neon-lit nightlife and primary hues to the blend. Bag-laden shoppers vie for curb space with street jugglers and vendors. Zen-inspired Hotel Omm offers a chance to flee the chaos of Gaudi and Gucci, offering a sanctuary of peacefulness where stepping into the ultra-chic lobby is to enter a meditative state.

Designed by architect Juli Capella to offer sleek and ambient city space, the Hotel Omm attracts a cool clientele who are hell-bent on chilling out. High above Barcelona's madding crowds in trendy Paseo de Gracia, a funky rooftop pool provides awesome views. Its Michelin-starred restaurant Moo and hip bar Moodern may be permanently full but this shouldn't put you off. Style is paramount at Hotel Omm where a clever jigsaw design pays homage to clutter-and-noise-free innovation. Even

the rowdiest fashion-forward crowd is barely audible, such are the acoustics. Vast swathes of natural light flood the building, circumnavigating snug enclaves illuminated by mellow lamp glow. Muted earth tones are beautifully contrasted with lacquered crimson detail in a quirky twist on minimalist Asian chic.

In the sweet-smelling Spaciomm Spa, all stresses and strains are banished as you are swaddled in super-soft kimonos and serenaded by tumbling waterfall cascades close to to Jacuzzis, pools, Turkish baths, a steam room, sauna, ice fountain and gravity room. Perfect-pitch wind chimes are suitably soporific and have helped to sooth the furrowed brows of an A-list jet-set crowd that includes Natalie Portman, Joan Branson and numerous faces from Barcelona's arts elite. An à la carte menu of therapies reads like an upscale Manhattan cocktail bar. As befitting an Asian-styled spa, several treatments centre on ancient Eastern health philosophies such as shiatsu and Ayurvedic massage. Keen to simply lounge around? Then cosy up in the Spaciomm's stylish relaxation area where reclined steel Jacuzzi chairs offer the decadence of sleepy peacefulness close to a fizzing Champagne fountain.

CONTACT
Hotel Omm
Tel: +34 934 454 000
Fax: +34 934 454 004
www.hotelomm.es

Catalonia Tourist Office
Email: turistex@correu.gencat.es
Tel: +34 93 484 97 55
Fax: +34 93 484 98 20
www.gencat.net

Cuddle up by a very modern fireside in the Hotel Omm.

008 LANZAROTE

CONTACTS
Holistic Holidays at Villa Iris
Tel: +44 (0)20 8123 9250 (UK)
Tel: +34 928 524 216
www.hoho.co.uk

*Practising yoga as a couple
can enhance trust and
communication.*

Derived from the Sanskrit root '*yuj*', meaning 'to join', yoga has important connotations when it comes to strengthening romantic ties. As a couple, yoga needn't purely be enjoyed as two separate individuals – but can be practised together, adding a new dimension to a relationship's depth and spiritual growth. Couples seeking ways to enjoy a greater bond can use yoga to feel closer to each other, physically and mentally. If all this sounds a bit New Age then fear not. Rather than a far-fetched hippy fad, so-called Couples Yoga is a healthy, new and fun way to spend time with your partner. Based on the ethos that all things are interdependent, exercise and rest are viewed as essential for vibrant health. Laughter and play are life's fountains of youth, so sessions are suitably packed with giggles, while trust and communication are focused on through touch. 'Somebody becomes closer and dearer to you as you understand them better', explains yoga guru Sadhguru Jaggi Vasudev. 'Then you enjoy the greater closeness.'

As a core component of all romantic relationships, touch is a binding force. It exchanges energy, allows auras to blend together and unite. Couples Yoga uses prolonged touch with locked eyes to maximise that vital 'connection'. Deep-breath inhalation, linked hands and bodies positioned just a breath apart pre-empt a series of slow yoga poses (asanas). Then there is a deep embrace. Many yogic teachings fuse feng shui principals into their couple programmes to strengthen energy fields, emotions and attraction. Love, it is taught, adjusts its strength according to an environment – driving Cupid away in cluttered surroundings where negative colours prevail.

At the Villa Iris Yoga Retreat on the island of Lanzarote warm rose-pinks, salmon-reds and soft coral tones mix with towering plants, ferns and flowers, an auspicious mix that offers lasting love, according to Feng Shui. Curved pebble pathways allow positive Ch'i to flow more easily with an open front garden (Yang) and a private rear green space (Yin) dotted with stone sundials, carved rock statues, stepping-stones, flickering fibre-optic lanterns and melodic wind chimes. Reiki, massage, meditation and shiatsu are all close at hand as is a fine organic menu using local produce. Villa Iris also manages to achieve that delicate balance of personal space and kindred company – and a finer setting in which to achieve a conspicuous transformation in togetherness is hard to imagine.

CONTACT
Tablao Cardenal
Tel: +34 957 483 320
www.tablocardenal.com

La Buleria
Tel: +34 957 433 889

Mesón Flamenco La Bulería
Tel: +34 957 483 839

Dancing the sevillanas *in Cordoba – a whirl of colour and energy.*

CORDOBA

Dubbed Spain's City of Romance on account of its sensual music and dance tradition, Cordoba's flamenco scene is firmly entrenched in the city's cobblestone old quarter, Juderia. Daytime Cordoba is a relaxed affair of pigeon-scattered plazas, pavement cafes and snoozing street-corner traders. It is after dark that the city truly bursts into life as restaurants and bars fill and music begins to flow as freely as the wine. Vibrant, passionate, intense and flamboyant Cordoba celebrates the riches of everyday life with the evocative flavours of food, dance, art, rhythm and song. As befits a city of romance, lyrics of lost love – the heart of Cordoba's spirit – emanate from dozens of cosy bars, cafes and *terrazas* to tug at the heartstrings. Conversation and dance are both engaged in with passion, but rarely without liquid accompaniment in the *tabernas* (traditional style taverns), *cervecerias* (speciality beer bars), *cocterlerias* (cocktail bars) and *bares de copas* (serving speciality spirits) city-wide. Unassuming, dimly lit doorways reveal stunning traditional tile-work, boldly painted ceramic murals, scrubbed wooden floors and lime-washed walls.

There is a joke in Cordoba that the day begins at 10pm when the lights dim, clubs open and crowds swell into the city. Traditional flamenco has its time now, stirring Cordoba with an intoxicating energy of whirling colour and the firecracker sound of heels on tile. Young and old radiate to the short, sharp claps as soulful cries rise above the music with a resonance that burrows deep into night. A dance of exuberance and intensity, the gypsy-originated flamenco rejects formality, preferring the freedom of improvised movements to mirror the mood of the moment. A strumming guitar follows the rhythms as dancers take to the floor with chins perfectly poised and arms aloft. A dance genre characterized by rapid passages and audible footwork, flamenco is thought to derive from the Arabic music traditions of Moorish times. In Cordoba, flamenco is the dance of the people with visitor participation welcomed by encouraging stamps and shouts. Simply allow your body to feel the *compás* (rhythm) rather than mechanically counting the beats. Close your eyes and yield to the escalating syncopated tempo of raw emotion, joy, passion and mournful lament.

CONTACT
Hotel Barceló Pueblo Park
Tel: +44 (0)800 4227 2356 (UK)
www.barcelopueblopark.com

Enjoy delicious chocolate-based spa treatments to put you in the mood for love.

MALLORCA

Most of us, at some time or another, have craved the velvety pleasures of chocolate. Medical evidence suggests that to deny this occasional indulgence is to miss out on one of the pleasures of life itself – not to mention good health. While these centre on chocolate's non-ingested forms, reports have attested to significant benefits to wellbeing. Beauty experts are also increasingly confirming that skin can never have too much chocolate as long as it is slathered on rather than ingested.

So why do we have such a love affair with chocolate? Well, the answer could lie in Phenylethylamine (PEA), a constituent of chocolate, and also a chemical found in the brain that rises as we experience joy and pleasure. Although many foods contain PEA, chocolate is loaded with it, so every time we allow a praline to tantalise our taste-buds we raise our levels to a stratospheric high. Our dermal rate of absorption suggests that this feel-good factor is transported to our brains during chocolate-laden spa therapies. Not only that, but once our face, body, hands and feet are layered in creamy chocolate our skin shows sure signs of obvious repair.

Cocoa beans, from which chocolate is made, are high in antioxidant phenolic phytochemicals (polyphenols), so high in fact that cocoa actually has higher antioxidant potential than green tea or red wine.

Native to Central and South America, cocoa was first brought to Europe via Spain by Hernando Cortez in the 1500s. Today, the Spanish connection prevails at the Hotel Barcelo Pueblo Park in the heart of Palma beach, Mallorca, where spa-goers are pampered with a decadent chocolate splurge. Indulge in delicious treatments, from a body peel with dark chocolate flakes, or a wrap with hot chocolate sauce, to a massage with chocolate and espresso-truffle oil. Chocolate is hand-blended into a thick emulsion with an essential oil, from rosewood and mandarin for rejuvenation, sandalwood and ylang ylang for relaxing, and grapefruit and clary sage for healing, filling the treatment room with a fulsome, mouthwatering aroma. Not only does cocoa beautifully nourish skin, making it super-soft, but it also boosts serotonin levels and feel-good endorphins to leave you in a happy state of mind. As the chocolately properties penetrate the skin you'll feel truly divine and smell good enough to eat. All this without adding an inch to your waistline – unless, that is, you inadvertently lick your lips.

ALICANTE

According to Chinese cosmology, the central concept of Yin and Yang relates to 'unity in duality': the binding of opposing forces. Once an equilibrium has been attained, the mind, body and soul reap the rewards of optimum wellness: the goal of Oriental health philosophies.

From the outside, the SHA Wellness Clinic wouldn't look out of place in New York City with its contemporary East-meets-West architecture and ultra-chic urban decor. Step inside and the tranquillity of the Zen-inspired interior exudes a peacefulness that transports you to the East in a state-of-the-art facility dedicated to longevity, agelessness and restorative R&R. The building itself is nestled between the sea and the magical green mountains, close to the secluded El Albir beach on the Mediterranean Coast.

At the heart of the SHA Wellness philosophy is the age-old health concept of a macrobiotic diet, a grain-based food regime supplemented with vegetables and pulses in which highly processed and refined produce is avoided. SHA has been developed with health guru George Ohsawa, a macrobiotic expert. Comprised of five striking individual buildings, the centre is straddled by interconnecting bridges over Zen gardens, lily-topped pools and bloom-filled chill-out zones.

Geared very much towards couples, SHA has 93 suites with private balconies and terraces, some with romantic Jacuzzis and small kitchens for in-room dining. Organic produce is used to help rid the body of toxins, cleansing the mind for a better balance of spirit, mind and body.

As well as medical consultations, personalised diets, talks, meditation and yoga, the SHA facility is home to a celebrated spa. Therapies here go beyond relaxation for far-reaching therapeutic benefits, from hydrotherapy and Asian-inspired touch therapies to detoxifying treatments. Practical advice looks at individual health goals to assess ways of improving physical health and achieving a new level of spiritual awareness. The SHA has positioned itself alongside India's Ananda in the Himalayas and Shanti Ananda Maurice in Mauritius – both great cradles of health and fine wellness models. A pioneering anti-stress and anti-ageing programme runs under the expert gaze of renowned Russian neurologist and longevity guru Sergey I. Surkov. Meditation classes follow thousand-year-old teachings to help couples reach beyond the conditioned 'thinking' mind. Once a deeper state of relaxation is achieved and the Yin-Yang balance restored, energy stores are free to heal mind, body and soul.

CONTACT
SHA Wellness Clinic
Tel +34 902 995 335
Fax: +34 966 864 528
Email: info@shawellnessclinic.com
www.shawellnessclinic.com

The SHA Wellness Clinic is the perfect place to enjoy Zen-inspired therapies.

GRANADA

CONTACT
Hotel Alhambra Palace
Tel: +34 958 22 14 68
Fax: +34 958 22 64 04
Email: reservas@
h-alhambrapalace.es
www.h-alhambrapalace.es

When Grace Kelly and her Prince Charming honeymooned in the 15th-century splendour of Granada's Moorish Alhambra Palace in the 1950s – following a fairytale ceremony in which the bride wore a stunning silk taffeta dress paired with a 70-metre (231-ft) tulle veil – the world's gaze turned to its romantic grandeur. With her new husband Prince Rainier, Grace embodied the dazzling radiance of a starry-eyed romantic dream as she tripped around the Alhambra Palace – Spain's Moorish jewel and Granada's glittering architectural treasure.

Built on a hilly terrace on Granada's southeastern edge, the Alhambra (meaning 'the red one') is the opulent former residence of the city's royal court under Arabic rule. A masterpiece of Spanish-Islamic architecture, the building is a celebration of ornamentation boasting impossibly intricate patterns of swirling vines and Arabic script interwoven onto gilt-laden panels of rich crimsons, black, blues and gold. Stucco pillars, coloured tiles, turrets, domes and spires characterise this stronghold of the Moorish Kings. Wrapped in a mile-long protective wall, the fortress had the capacity for forty thousand men and today forms the centrepiece of Granada's aura of magical romance. Stroll through resplendent gardens of enchanted pools and fountains to the Parador de San Francisco, Granada's 15th century former convent, past ancient trees, huge arched windows and leafy, paved courtyards. Stay overnight and request a room overlooking the gardens for a truly unforgettable romantic vista across the rose bushes, orange trees and myrtles. Moorish poets wrote of 'a pearl set in emeralds' in reference to the palace's alabaster stone and lush, green garden setting. Listen to nightingales in the moonlight to the gentle sounds of bubbling cascades amidst marble columns, horseshoe archways, exquisite mosaics and reflective pools.

As the inspiration for Manuel de Falla's evocative opera *El Romance de Granada*, the Alhambra Palace (*Qal'at al Hamr*) is the symbol of a city hand-crafted for romancing. Though lavish and grand in scale, Granada is not without its simple magic – few things are as memorable as watching the sun fade from the Mirador de San Nicolas as the city slowly illuminates the Alhambra in a spectacular golden glow. British composer Julian Anderson's *Alhambra Fantasy* symphony is similarly stirring, drawing on the gasp-inducing beauty of the palace as inspiration – a passionate composition drenched in heart-felt sentiment and spirited emotion.

The glorious Alhambra Palace – a Moorish jewel and the perfect setting for romance.

FRANCE

Almost the entire world has in some way been exposed to French influences, be it the wine, coffee and croissants, lavender fields or elegant châteaux. Chic, tree-lined Parisian boulevards, the sun-speckled vineyards of Burgundy and the sun-kissed beaches of Cannes embody the diversity of French culture. Mountains and hills cover vast swathes of the country including the mighty Alps, Pyrenees and Vosges. France is also famed for its sun-drenched Mediterranean coast: a sizzling summer beach destination and popular winter resort. As one the world's most beautiful cities, Paris, set in a sedimentary basin on the banks of the romantic River Seine, harbours fine Baroque architecture and world-class art galleries.

TIME DIFFERENCE GMT +1

TELEPHONE CODE +33

CURRENCY Euro

LANGUAGE French

POPULATION 61.5 milion

SIZE OF COUNTRY 547,030 sq km (213,342 sq miles)

CAPITAL Paris

WHEN TO GO Coastal regions sizzle in July and August while the French Alps in the southeast of the country attract skiers in their droves in winter months. Spring and autumn are ideal seasons for hiking, cycling, climbing and running.

TOURIST INFORMATION
Maison de la France (the French Tourist Board)
Tel: 09068 244 123
Email: info.uk@franceguide.com
www.franceguide.com

013

PARIS

CONTACTS
Paris Authentic 2CV Tours
Tel: +33 6 64 50 44 19
Email: paris@parisauthentic.com
www.parisauthentic.com

Tours cost from 160 euros
per couple.

The Swedish are renowned for sleek, contemporary design, the Italian's for sexy chic while stylish ingenuity is a German strongpoint. And the French? Well, just a glance at the Citroën 2CV casts a question mark over their design panache – a car so ugly that it is actually cute. Dubbed the Ugly Duckling of the Citroën world, the 2CV enjoys a cult following these days: the iconic, slightly gawky sex symbol of French motor vehicles. Hidden from the Nazis and manufactured for 42 years, the beloved 2CV has charmed the world for over a half a century. It boasts dozens of nicknames across the globe, from *jernseng* ('iron bedstead' in Norwegian), *la cabra* ('goat' in Spanish) and *chocolaterias* ('chocolate tin can' in Portuguese) to the rather unkind 'tin snail'. Today, millions of derivatives across 30 different models have been produced around the globe, spawning over 300 2CV automotive clubs and rallies worldwide. Not bad for something its own designer admitted looked like an umbrella on wheels.

Citroën unveiled the first 2CV at the prestigious Paris Salon in 1948, yet the original concept was a pre-war 1930s prototype developed in complete secrecy, codenamed TPV (*toute petite voiture*, simply meaning 'very small car'). Made from lightweight alloys, the early 2CV had a magnesium chassis and wheels. A canvas body stretched over a frame with seats that were no more than hammocks suspended from the roof. A set of added-on headlights gave it a nerdy, bug-eyed look, yet the French country folk adored the 2CV's go-anywhere suspension. Low earners loved its unbeatable price and even snooty Parisians considered the 600 kg (1,326 lb) design revolution beyond fashion. First produced only in grey, other colours followed, representing one of just a few changes made to Pierre Boulanger's original design over the years.

Designed to carry four averagely-proportioned adults wearing their Sunday-best hats, this space-efficient front-wheel-drive motor boasts a top speed of 60 kph (37 mph). Economical to run and cheap to maintain, it achieves a fuel consumption of 3 litres per 100 km (⅔ gallon per 62 miles); a 3-speed gear box is equipped with a

supercharger peg that acts as a fourth gear. It is capable of running on the worst of roads, of being driven by a debutante, and is reassuringly comfy. Even the removable back seats doubled up as a handy picnic bench on a country jaunt over *Le Weekend*. Yet its proudest boast was that the 2CV was roomy enough for 50 kg (111 lbs) of potatoes and able to transport a basket of eggs over a freshly ploughed field without a single breakage – no mean feat.

Today, the 2CV is cherished by millions for its awkward, kookily romantic looks and compact, unworldly shape. For a non-streamlined design, it

delivers a ride that is incredibly smooth with a well damped suspension that is couch-like rather than springy. It is a cosy car: somehow warm, cuddly and forgiving with more heart than a mere 'tin snail' should rightly possess. The BBC Top Gear programme's Jeremy Clarkson may have written the 2CV off as a 'weedy, useless little engine', but the *Deux Chevaux* (as the French call it, meaning 'two horses') remains the most quintessentially French vehicle to trundle the roads – an automotive that epitomizes Gallic charm. Even in Paris, a fleet of 2CVs offers two-person sightseeing trips to tourists keen to explore the city in France's cosiest and most iconic four-wheeled, metal cocoon. Somehow the romantic character of the city is heightened by a 2CV journey along the old Parisian streets which speak of another era. Available in blue, white and red, Authentic Paris' wonderfully cared for Ugly Ducklings offer a rare nostalgic treat around Notre Dame and the tree-lined Champs Elysées in true French automotive style. Booking a 'Romantic Paris' tour adds some nice additional touches for couples keen to snuggle up in this comically soft, coil-sprung motor – including heart-warming tales of candlelit Paris from a beret-wearing chauffeur.

Duke, debutante or just plain 'deux', find romance on the streets of Paris in this cutest of cars.

014

CONTACT
Atelier de Cuisine Gastronomique
Tel: +33 4 78 35 06 07
Email: infos@cuisinedechef.com
www.cuisinedechef.com

Lyon Tourism Board
Tel: +33 4 72 77 69 69
Email: info@lyon-france.com
www.en.lyon-france.com

Paul Bocuse Institute
Tel: +33 4 72 18 02 20
Email: contact@institut
paulbocuse.com
www.institutpaulbocuse.com

*Mouthwatering dishes abound
in France's gastronomic capital.*

LYON

Gallic culinary history is riddled with salacious analogies that draw juicy parallels between food and sexual pleasure. Over the centuries, millions of carefully crafted culinary fusions have been ingested in pursuit of digestive ecstasy: a passionate pastime worshipped and adored for its gratifying sensory power. Gastronomic know-how is much like sexual prowess, according to Jim Kar, author of *If Food is Love, Cooking is Foreplay*. With these erotic analogies between bed and plate, it is little wonder so many Gallic menus read like an aphrodisiac banquet. It may also explain why the pans of France boil over in an orgy of culinary lust. Food and love are close cousins; our enjoyment of both depends on who else comes to the table. Craving, consummation and satiation: the comparisons are legion in a nation of chefs with insatiable appetites for pleasure. We stare and lick our lips, before yielding to the French passion of gastronomy. In Lyon, this is gourmet *amour*, where food fantasies are readily indulged.

As France's gastronomic capital, Lyon owes much to the 19th-century *Mères* culinary tradition, originated by female cooks in times gone by but now largely practiced by men. Paul Bocuse, the world-renowned Lyon chef, started out with *mère* Brazier while other famous *mères* include *la mère*

Blanc, *la mère* Fillioux, *la mère* Poupon and *la mère* Léa, la grande Marcelle. In this gastronomic heartland every meal and snack is a sensuous union of fresh produce, herbs and spices combined in mouth-watering matrimony: Bresse poultry with vegetables from the Ain plain; cheese from Dauphiné and Ardèche with Beaujolais, Côtes du Rhône, Dugey and Burgundy wines; and Dombes pike and carp with fruit from les Monts du Lyonnais and the Rhone valley. Feast on local salami, *rosette*, *quenelles* and *andouillette* sausages together with locally made chocolates and cream.

Dozens of open-air markets and covered food halls across Lyon offer a chance to sample the goods, such as those in Part-Dieu, or the small Halles de la Martinière or des Brotteaux. Be prepared for stallholders to point out the aphrodisiacal qualities of everything in your basket, from that libido-boosting bunch of celery, the fertility-enhancing pomegranate, a vigour-rejuvenating peach, some testosterone-increasing grains and a bulb of arousal-boosting garlic, together with honeymoon favourites, oysters and caviar. Lyon's tempting array of world-class eateries ranges from simple local *bouchons* (traditional bistros) to restaurants owned by renowned chefs, such as gastronomic maestro Paul Bocuse, who has wooed foodies across the planet with a culinary frisson of exotic influences. Tourists keen to indulge a passion for French food can take a daily class at Chef Jean-Marc Villard's world famous cooking school where, in hands-on style, he promises to deliver the pinnacle of pleasure on a plate.

Villard's classes take place in his professional teaching kitchen built in his gorgeous garden in Champagne au Mont d'Or, about 10 minutes from Lyon's bustling centre. This gregarious gourmet is a seductive purveyor of culinary secrets and imparts tips and *savoir faire* with a wink of the eye and a knowing smile. He prefers small groups, and often attracts couples keen to expand their kitchen repertoire. The style is relaxed and informal with Villard open and adaptable to individual requirements. A finalist in the Best Professionals of France (2000), he boasts a long list of accomplishments at Michelin-starred restaurants and held the post of chef-professor for a decade at the Ecole des Arts Culinaires et de l'Hôtellerie, now the *Paul Bocuse* Institute. Choose from a cooking lesson only or add on an early morning gastronomic experience that allows a glimpse into Villard's world of local suppliers, from meat and poultry merchants to fish, vegetable, fruit, wine and herb markets. In an atmosphere of conviviality, would-be chefs gather at Villard's kitchen at 9am where they are togged out in aprons and primed for action. Aptly hot and sweaty (despite air-conditioning), Jean-Marc Villard whips up a gourmet frenzy with true Gallic passion and is rapturous about Lyon's culinary tradition. Sessions culminate in a menu tasting that allows participants to devour dishes on a pretty, creeper-clad outdoor terrace, with a glass of wine to toast life, loves – and Lyon.

Learn to cook up an enticing gastronomic storm with a Michelin-starred chef.

015

CONTACTS
Les Source de Caudalie
Tel: 00800 4429 2424 (European free
call number)
www.sources-caudalie.com

Château Smith Haut Lafitte
Tel: +33 5 57 83 11 22
Fax: +33 5 57 83 11 21
www.smith-haut-lafitte.com

Bordeaux Tourism
Tel: +33 5 56 00 66 00
Fax: +33 5 56 00 66 01
www.bordeaux-tourisme.com

*Enjoy a full-bodied vin
experience before relaxing
in one of Les Sources de
Caudalie's beautiful bedrooms.*

BORDEAUX

No other libation is as synonymous with *amour* as wine, the so-called Nectar of the Gods. Enjoying sultry Sauternes or sumptuous Sangiovese can help couples spark sensual chemistry, according to *romancetips.com*, while *romanceclass.com* swears by mellow mood-enhancer, Merlot. In France, wine spa Les Sources de Caudalie has taken wine to another level, preparing vintages in which to bathe the body and nourish the spirit. No part of the vine is wasted, from the leaves, skins and juice to the seeds, sediment and extracts. Given what a single glass can achieve, heaven knows what a top-to-toe soaking with robust Bordeaux in France's wine capital could lead to. With deep, luxurious tubs made for two, the mind can only boggle.

Apparently, the Romans doused themselves in wine in the name of beauty, so the concept of Les Sources de Caudalie, albeit wholly unique, isn't new. At the 72-hectare, 18th-century Château Smith Haut Lafitte, modern winemaking techniques combine with age-old traditional methods using organic compost. Vines rich in

nutrient-heavy polyphenols are packed with free radicals. Grape pulp, stalks and seeds are all powerful detoxifiers with anti-ageing properties around 10,000 times stronger than Vitamin E. Wine-lovers can revel in a *dégustation extraordinaire* thanks to a 100 per cent Grape Therapy vinotherapie package. Over 35 wine-inspired lotions, potions, scrubs and tonics include the sumptuous oils created by husband and wife team Mathilde and Bertrand Thomas, under the motto *Salus per Vinum*, (meaning 'Healthy Living through Grapes').

In France, forgoing the finer things in life is practically sacrilegious, even in a health spa; denial and deprivation are certainly alien concepts at Les Source de Caudalie, where rejuvenation takes many forms. Aside from the Bordeaux Barrel Baths, Merlot Wraps and Red Vine Detoxifying Teas, there's an ultra-romantic, candle-lit, Michelin-star restaurant with a 13,000-bottle cellar (complete with wine-tasting sessions) to ensure every aspect of the the the grape's sophistication is truly relished.

LIMOGES

At one time, to openly discuss caricature as 'art' was considered a silly presumption worthy of ridicule. Today, these hand-drawn, whimsical sketches represent a highly regarded artistic genre, in which gentle mockery and fond affection interfuse. A centuries-old art form that experienced its first successes in the closed aristocratic circles of Paris, the art of the caricature portrait remains a long-standing French tradition. Drawing on the natural characteristics of the subject (large, puppy-dog eyes or crooked smile); acquired characteristics (facial expressions and mannerisms); and vanities (spectacles and hairstyle), a caricature distorts the essence of a person to create an easily identifiable visual likeness. While some caricaturists stretch that artistic embroidery to extremes, the prevailing style in France is kindly teasing. Like a photograph, hand-drawn caricature provides a commemorative snapshot of a cherished moment in time. Nowadays, France's caricaturists ply their ancient art amongst the county's boardwalk flower stalls and boulevards to offer unique, deeply-personal and treasured sentimental keepsakes that are sure to raise a smile.

Couples keen for an unconventional romantic portrait are increasingly turning to caricature as a medium as it can often better reflect the importance of humour in the life they share. The romantic sentiment is there, it just requires deciphering with subtlety more than overblown amplification. 'A sense of humour is *très importante* to a lasting marriage... *oui*?!' joke the artists at their easels. Less formal than a stuffy engagement photo and more personal than a standard wedding announcement, an off-the-wall illustration can capture the essence of a fun-loving couple in humorous terms.

Some of France's greatest caricaturists include Charles Philipon, owner of the magazine *La Caricature*, who pushed satire to the limits in the 1800s. In the 1900s, Comte Amadee de Noe, better known as Cham, reflected his eccentric noble lineage in his artistry while Honoré Daumier (1808–1879) is considered to be a pioneer of the modern caricature style. Even Claude Monet, an

artist better known for his expressive canvasses, was a passionate caricaturist, sketching family and friends for mutual amusement during celebrations at his home. Today, Europe's largest Festival of Caricature is held at St Just le Martel, just to the east of Limoges. During the week-long October event, visitors can commission works and buy one-off sketches from Frances's most prized illustrators who draw in friendly competition for a fittingly unconventional award – a fully-grown cow.

CONTACT
St Just Le Martel Cartoon Festival
Tel: +33 5 55 09 26 70
Fax: +33 5 55 09 26 33
www.st-just.com

A caricature drawing makes a fun memento.

017

LOIRE

CONTACT
Château Villandry
Tel: +33 2 47 50 02 09
Fax: +33 2 47 50 12
Email: info@chateauvillandry.com
www.chateauvillandry.com

With its annual 'Rendezvous in the Gardens' and Candlelit Garden Evenings, the Château de Villandry is no stranger to romance. Since its construction in 1536, as one of the last Loire Valley Renaissance-era châteaux, Villandry was built by Jean le Breton, a former ambassador to Italy, who had developed a passion for the art of romantic gardens whilst studying in Rome.

Today the château's exquisite, re-laid 16th century parterres continue to draw gasps from visitors to this extensive, geometric garden punctuated by clipped box hedges and neatly trimmed, low-lying shrubs. Particularly resplendent are the stunning displays of varicoloured year-round blooms planted on two stepped terraces. Combining the style of a French monastic garden with Italianate models like those depicted in Du Cerceau etchings, these flowered checkerboards are truly breathtaking – and guaranteed to make every green-thumbed visitor weak at the knees.

Set on the banks of the Cher River and flanked by a cliffside pathway, the gardens of the Château de Villandry have been crafted around the flow of water, beginning in a large basin toward the rear of the grounds. Individually created stepped gardens are broken by bridges and small waterfalls, ringed by a canal-fed moat and centred on a main courtyard. A handsome potager sits amongst a vast, embroidery-like carpet of rare and colourful flowers. Fragrant herbs form a tufted rug beneath a boulevard of 1,500 perfectly manicured mature trees. Pungent spices hide amongst a decorative kitchen garden, segmented into perfect squares by fruit tree borders and vegetable beds, whilst saplings gaze up at vast canopies amidst triangular lawns and precisely cut box sculptures. A swan-filled ornamental lake offers subdued calm amongst the vibrancy and colour of the rest of the garden, a spectacle that is enhanced during the Château's celebrated festivals when myriad lanterns adorn pebbled pathways and pergolas.

Romantics keen to whisper sweet nothings amongst the hedgerows should visit during the French lunchtime (12–2pm). The blissful seclusion offered by the Château's leafy, labyrinthine paths makes it the perfect spot for *amour*. Stroll across the gardens dedicated to adoration, as well as ornamental terraces displaying rich depictions of the ancient symbols of chivalric love. Pass by the dahlia-planted hearts of the Tender Love area before pausing amongst the blooms of the Passionate Love garden. Delight in a voyage of romance where floral odes to the facets of love have blossomed over many centuries past.

The picture-perfect potager at Château Villandry; punctuated by fountains and shielded by formal hedges, this is a true garden of romance.

CONTACT
Bourgogne Tourisme
Tel: +33 3 80 28 02 80
Fax: +33 3 80 28 03 00
www.burgundy-tourism.com

Bateau Who Knows
Tel: + 33 611 853 249 /
+44 (0)7766 455 933
Email: contact@charterbarge.com
www.charterbarge.com

Create your own tales from the riverbank; indulge in a little romance as you glide lazily past an ever-changing vista.

BURGUNDY

Once you allow yourself to become accustomed to travelling at a snail's pace, it is a liberating experience, which is why journeying by barge is unbeatably genteel, especially when you're spared all the chores. This is the case aboard the *Bateau Who Knows*: a captained vessel that travels the narrow canals and rivers of Burgundy (Bourgogne) at a sedate 5 kph (3 mph). The *Who Knows*' name is a literal translation of the Dutch '*Wie Zalt Weten*', giving a clue as to the past life of this 1930's Dutch-built grain ferry. Now English-owned, the nomadic *Who Knows* is content to meander along Burgundy's centuries-old waterways, her distinctive dark wood panelling and sleek, curvaceous shape ensuring she is one of the finest classic cruisers in France. Pretty stone villages, medieval châteaux, ancient market towns and lily-topped reservoirs are just a few of the canalside attractions. Raise a glass to the upcoming vintage as you pass wine terraces at a leisurely pace. Time is a plentiful luxury on this unhurried, almost trance-like voyage in a region where impeccable wines and a grandiose history combine to much aplomb.

Routes meander around the waterways of the Ouche Valley past a land of Roman-era bridges, half-timbered houses, Cistercian monasteries and romantic fortified castles perched high above the canal. Numerous lock transits allow ample opportunities to disembark for a stroll along the tow path – on foot or on two wheels. Watching the world glide by is a much-underrated pursuit, but one that is fully enjoyed amid steep-sided riverbanks and thick deciduous forest where wild boar and deer roam. Visit the 15th-century wine presses of Clos du Vougeot and the producers of Nuits Saint Georges before marvelling at cellars at Patriarche Pere et Fils – home to 4 million bottles.

The *Who Knows*' three air-conditioned double cabins are equipped with en-suite shower rooms, with a comfortable lounge, library and music room on board. A 30 sq m (323 sq ft) contemporary stainless steel canopy complements an adjoining suntrap. Dine on dishes from France's gastronomic hinterland, cooked using fresh local produce, sample fine wines and enjoy traditional recipes with baskets of fresh crusty bread delivered each day. Highlights include Burgundian *oeufs en meurette* (eggs poached in red wine with bacon), washed down with a fine Côte de Beaune, Chablis, Côte de Nuits, Pouilly Fuissé or Mâcon and accompanied by a side order of ever-changing views.

019

CONTACT
Château d'Etoges
Tel: + 33 3 26 59 30 08
Fax: +33 3 26 59 35 57
Email: contact@etoges.com
www.chateau-etoges.com

Aube en Champagne Tourist Board
Tel: +33 3 25 42 50 00
Fax: +33 33 3 25 42 50 88
Email: bonjour@aube-
champagne.com
www.aube-champagne.co.uk

*Put the fizz back at the
gorgeous Château d'Etoges.*

CHAMPAGNE

Champagne's delicate bubbles are symbolic of love, joy and union – just a single, sparkling sip is so often a tantalizing prelude to passion and promise. French historian Geneviève Dévignes declared it an 'inseparable companion of joyous heavenly events, crown of festivities and special celebrations... symbol of friendship... holy dedication to love', a sentiment shared by friends and lovers across the globe. In no place is this affection greater than in France's fabled Champagne Country where 270 local producers create the finest fizz on the planet. Yet far from the pretentious grandeur of Reim's Rue de Champagne lie clusters of tiny, family-owned small producers in vine-trimmed, cobbled villages set amidst sunflower fields. The region's rich soil nurtures carpets of vines laden with fruit that sweep down to verdant wildflower meadows. Deep forests rim a succession of plunging, steep-sided valleys famous for their Grand Cru vineyards and impeccable Pinot Noir grapes.

Few settings in Champagne are as resplendent as the Château d'Etoges, a magnificent, turreted 17th-century former staging post for journeying French monarchs and nobility. Enchanting sparkling fountains, swan-filled moats and sumptuous, Chandelier–filled drawing rooms have played host to Louis XIV and Napoleon's courtiers. Now, family-owned for over a century, the Château d'Etoges continues to uphold the tradition of a Royal welcome, rolling out the red carpet for every honoured guest. Grand, grey-stone towers sit amongst expansive formal gardens dotted with neat hedges, whilst a pretty surrounding village of winemakers and vineyards ensures the famous *Côte des Blancs* is always close at hand. Keen for a bubble-filled kick from Champagne? Then look out for a signs reading *dégustation*, for a tongue-tingling tasting session extraordinaire. Choose from a lavish, Champagne-sipping soirée or a simply opt to share a bottle on the bobbing waters of the moat in a rowing boat for two. Pop a cork at sunset for a romantic sortie as you glide under low-lying bridges overlooked by round towers and soaring steeples.

BRITTANY

Brittany may have been synonymous for generations with its crisp apple cider, but in recent years it has been the region's less appetizing liquid that has attracted high praise. So-called 'sea therapy' using Brittany's mineral-rich seawater has been heralded for its health-giving benefits. Not that extolling the virtues of saltwater is anything new: the Greeks and Romans swore by seawater cleansing and the sea has been used in healing since ancient times.

Said to contain 120 chemical compounds in the form of salts and dissolved gas, seawater is a powerful natural detoxifier. Through osmosis, the skin absorbs nitrogen, oxygen and helium, plus over 50 different mineral particles, trace elements and negative ions during seawater therapy. Today, Brittany's coastal waters have been incorporated into a range of well-being therapies, from marine mud and algae treatments to hydrotherapy, massage and lymphatic drainage. Restorative and rebalancing, salt water is also hailed as a bodily rejuvenator that enhances vitality, augments physical strength and agility and gives energy a boost. Many also believe that Brittany's fresh sea air is laced with untold curative benefits so walking the shoreline, inhaling deeply, allows the capillaries to deliver minerals directly to the bloodstream.

Meaning *Sanitas Per Aquum* (health through water) from which the acronym was derived, the spa was originally created using only the curative powers of Mother Nature. Thalassotherapy centres and spas are strung along the coastline from Mont St-Michel to La Baule. Most, like the Thalasso Douarnenez, boast a vast number of seawater therapies, many focusing on stress-free relaxation – the perfect foundation for romance.

Almost every marine-inspired beauty product range on the planet uses seaweed from Brittany's shores. More than 50,000 tonnes per annum is collected from the pollution-free coast. Once harvested, it is transformed from its natural state into a more absorbable product, taking care not to alter its health-giving properties in the process. When applied to the body, this rich source of potassium, magnesium, amino acids and iodine helps establish nervous and muscular equilibrium

– so the benefits are far from merely cosmetic. One of the most popular body therapies uses a masque of algae, marine mud and seaweed. After being first softened with warm seawater and coarse salt grains, the skin is lavished in the mixture and wrapped in clingfilm. After being left to lie under a heated blanket, the client is cleansed in a cool marine shower before being gently massaged and moisturized. Just as relaxing are Brittany's expansive scenic views that encapsulate it's craggy, aquatic landscape rich in marine birds and wildlife.

CONTACT
Thalasso Douarnenez
Tel: +33 8 25 00 42 30
Fax: +33 2 98 74 45 68
www.thalasso.com

A tourist office brochure provides an indispensable guide to what's what across the region – simply call 0800 085 7739 (UK) and ask for a copy.

A glorious sunset in the Finistère region of Brittany.

021

CONTACT
Claude Monet Foundation
Tel: +33 2 32 51 28 21
Fax: +33 2 32 51 54 18
Email: contact@fondation-monet.com
www.fondation-monet.com

A kaleidescope of colours at Monet's gardens at Giverny.

NORMANDY

To journey through Claude Monet's dazzling, bloom-filled gardens at Giverny is to understand his passion for heart-stirringly vivid colour. For this living, growing, floral canvas boasts an extraordinary combination of hues: a trademark of this great initiator of the evocative Impressionist style of painting. Weeping willows trail over delicate wooden bridges set amidst a blaze of bold violet-blues tempered by green lilies and golden flecks. Soft cherry pinks, mellow mauves and inky purples morph into pewter shadows while crimson poppies tumble across the warm amber hayfields that surround the gardens. Depicting love and the natural world, Monet was inspired by the sensual splashes of colour that enveloped him, from the joyous sunshine of summer and autumn's fallen leaves to the bleakness and wonderment of winter. Life, love and romance were his favourite themes. Like his oils, plants were Monet's artistic tools of the trade with the bare soil in his gardens at Giverny his canvas. Mixing his colours became a love-fuelled obsession that transcended art: 'More than anything else, I must have flowers, always, always...', he wrote.

Monet's adoration of colour is evident throughout his five-acre garden. Using vibrant shrubs for year-round colour and texture, he experimented with bulbs, perennials and annuals from all over the world. Monet loved the hazy, shimmering effect of colour and created numerous series of flower-stuffed geometric beds and rose-covered arches. By selecting plants that swayed and fluttered in the breeze, Monet created movement, evident in a rippling tide of Oriental poppies that punctuate a sea of cosmos. A sophisticated palette daubed with blue, pink, yellow, red, green and silver owed its beauty to bearded irises, daisies, gladioli, hollyhocks, pansies, black violas, nasturtiums, cleome, phlox, forget-me-nots, bluebells, wallflowers, pinks, sage and sunflowers. Only black had no place in his garden, or his art.

Monet's brushwork shows determination and rigorous observation, much like that of Edouard Manet, whose work in the 1860s proved a guiding influence to Impressionists. As a means of capturing the delicate colours he so cherished, Monet crafted beautiful injections of light and contrast in his canvasses, conveying the subtle essence of nature in the style of truly romantic art. He also demonstrated pure luminosity in his 19th-century gardens, dividing the planted areas into a flower-filled Clos Normand garden and a Japanese-inspired water garden. Since Monet's death in 1926, these gardens have been open to the public. Today over half a million visitors a years from all over the world pay homage to Monet's irrepressible affection for love, life, nature – and colour.

PAU

Hot air ballooning enjoys a storied tradition in The Pyrenees, offering some of Europe's finest panoramas against a magnificent backdrop of jagged mountains. Sweeping plateaux, undulating countryside, high bluffs and ragged spits boast extraordinary flora and fauna. Innumerable and large rocky protrusions run parallel to the spiny ridges while the rolling folds of the landscape form crumbled meadows in the flower-scattered foothills beneath. Light gusts offer the perfect propulsion for balloon travel, aiding Jesus Fernandez Duro to make the first balloon-powered crossing of the Pyrénées in 1906. Today, the grounds of the beautiful, vine-cloaked 15th-century Cistercian Abbaye de l'Escaladieu serves as a romantic launch point for balloon explorations of the mountains, allowing a scenic ascent over the confluence of the Luz and Aroos Rivers near the castle of Mauvezin. Getting off the ground requires a pilot to connect propane tanks to the burners. Once the valve is switched on, a flame jettisons into the silken envelope as it slowly inflates to a swell. Ropes untied, a bumpy take-off preludes a weightless rise skyward, accompanied by a gaseous roar as the balloon enters its timeless, floating state. High above the ancient pilgrims' route to Santiago de Compostela, the romance of a weightless world unfolds as do the gasp-inducing views.

Balloon travel provides the ultimate in joyously haphazard romantic journeying, embodying an exotic, unsystematic mode of exploration driven by a frisky breeze. Although a skilled pilot can influence the height of a hot-air balloon within centimetres, it is the wind that dictates direction. Few travel plans are as romantically fickle as those that rely on the whim of Mother Nature – and it is this liberating casting of fate that forms the bedrock of ballooning's romantic appeal. Skim across wooded Alpine thickets and wind-chiselled limestone crags at a leisurely 25 kph (16 mph). Cross boulder-strewn streams, rustic mountain villages, ancient Ibex trails and stone ledges covered in creeping scrub. When it is time to swap a cloudy puffball for solid ground, brace yourself for a jolt as you return to earth in a tufted meadow.

CONTACT
Aquitaine Montgolfières
Tel: +33 5 59 66 59 22 /
+33 6 80 34 30 34
Email: aquitaine.montgolfieres@
wanadoo.fr
www.aquitaine-montgolfieres.fr

Expect to pay around 300 euros for a romantic airborne soirée-for-two, with Champagne and a hand-tied floral bouquet available on request for an extra special touch.

Up, up and away: enjoy a romantic airbourne cruise over the French countryside.

023

RIQUEWIHR

CONTACTS
Régional du Tourism d'Alsace
Tel: +33 3 88 25 01 66
Fax: +33 3 88 52 17 06
Email: crt@tourisme-alsace.com
www.tourisme-alsace.com

Stroll narrow, storied streets in the medieval town of Riquewihr.

Riquewihr's medieval splendour draws involuntary gasps from first-time visitors as they approach on the gloriously vine-hemmed Rue de Vin. Nestled in a small valley in the foothills of the blue-green Vosges Mountains, Riquewihr remains an object of centuries-old wonderment, its narrow, cobbled streets brimming with charming buildings in a kaleidoscopic array of vivid hues. Unchanged since the Middle Ages, the half-timbered architecture has been painstakingly and sensitively preserved – and so, too, has the culture. Riquewihr's fusion of Gallic-Germanic traditions continues to dominate local heritage, from language to food and festivals, with every aspect of daily life revolving around the grape.

To discover France's most romantic town is to stroll its narrow alleys and uneven streets amidst a blaze of colour that positively glows from the building facades, from pale pink and faded blue to shades of violet, yellow and red. Leafy, paved courtyards, ancient stone wells and fresh-water fountains hide amongst the nooks and crannies.

Devoid of cars, bar the occasional delivery vehicle, it seems only fitting that Riquewihr's genteel beauty is uninterrupted by engine noise. Few towns are as picture-postcard idyllic, framed by fine historic monuments, just a stone's throw from Germany and the Rhine. Entwined couples meander slowly along the main street to retreat into secluded backstreets while others hold hands as they lift their eyes skyward to marvel at spires and clock towers. Climb up to the Dolder Tower, the town's 700-year-old highest point, to enjoy spectacular views across a checkerboard landscape of vine terraces, forests and ruins dotted with picturesque Gothic steeples and turrets. Peruse the Upper Gateway from the 16th and 17th centuries, the focal point of the outer ramparts, with double gates, portcullis, drawbridge and loopholes. Choose a peaceful, shaded spot to share a heart-shaped cinnamon cookie in the fortifications of this romantic medieval settlement, or sip a crisp sparking Crément at the cosy Au Cep de Vigne under jutting gables and Princess-worthy towers.

CONTACTS
Les Roulottes
Tel: +33 4 74 04 76 40
Email: ppatin@free.fr
www.lesroulottes.com

Open April to October only.

A restored gypsy caravan makes a snug romantic bolthole.

BEAUJOLAIS

France holds considerable nostalgic affection for the romance of a nomadic life on the road, spawning numerous works of fiction devoted to vagabond tales of journeying the nation's historic and storied terrain. Many centre on clichéd memories of 15th-century gypsy folklore, born out of horse-drawn bucolic roving by nomads, or Romanies. Colourful stories of cross-country roaming in painted wooden wagons captured the hearts and minds of those with a wanderlust and itchy feet. Today, only five traditional caravan-makers ply their trade in France, a fraction of those once engaged in this age-old gypsy craft. Most are hippies, like Pascal Pain and his wife Pascaline who, in a ramshackle workshop, build fine replica *roulottes* (caravans) to ancient designs.

With slavish passion, the couple also dote on three beautifully restored *roulottes*, dating back to the 1920s, 30s and 50s respectively. Each retains bags of original character intermingled with Bohemian road-warrior chic, with special features ranging from whimsical artwork depicting outlandish travel themes to hand-chiselled mirrors and carved woods. Warm, natural wooden tones meet bold vibrant hues adorned with flickering wall lights, mosaics, woven rugs and candles. This spirited decor complements some basic guest amenities, such as power, heating and running water. Roughly hewn wood epitomises a rugged, road-weary travellers' den, while colourful, rainbow-thread blankets cover comfy, log-built beds for sweet dreams under a starry sky.

La Roulotte des Amoureux (the Lovers' Caravan) sits in a secluded, wooded enclave hemmed by shrubs and is a favourite with lovers and honeymooning couples. Rickety wooden steps lead into a bubblegum-hued interior deliciously adorned in flowing, candy-pink drapes. Crimson and rose-coloured cushions lie scattered across a sumptuous bed swathed in cerise. Snug, warm and inviting, this cocoon-like love shack can be super-heated (for 3 Euros per day) to ensure maximum smooch-factor. Grand candelabras illuminate this most love-inspired setting where a rustic Beaujolais dinner can be served at your very own romantic, al fresco table for two. Simply pour a glass of Fleurie, squeeze two seats together amongst the garden blossom and allow the moonlight to work its magic.

025

Dedicated to love, Le Couvent nestles amidst the vineyards of Languedoc.

LANGUEDOC

Languedoc derives its name from the ancient tongue of a rich artistic culture that gave birth to the medieval ancestor of the modern notion of romantic love. It is often said that every stone in Languedoc has a story to tell, from the wild, rolling, sparsely populated wooded hills of Margeride and the gorges of the Tarn River to the limestone summits of the Causses. Pretty villages of stone cottages, robust fortresses, fairytale spires, châteaux and romantic follies have provided the perfect, light-drenched canvas for many painters through the ages. Collioure played host to the beginnings of Fauvism through Matisse and Derain; Céret is the home of Cubism, through Picasso, Braque, Herbin and Juan Gris, while Dali declared Perpignan 'the centre of the world'. Romance continues to thrive in Languedoc in its storied viniculture history – with exceptional domains steeped in myths of romance, pride and passion – amidst over 300,000 hectares of rolling vines that produce more wine than the whole of Australia.

For a romantic weekend break, consider the boutique hotel Le Couvent, a heavenly sanctuary away from the stresses of fast-paced modern life. Located in a setting that can only be described as idyllic, in the very heart of the Languedoc vineyards, Le Couvent is exclusively for adults and

a popular honeymoon retreat. As such, the hotel is a romance specialist, organising tailored menus for guests keen to enjoy romantic tête-à-têtes, and shopping for personalised gifts and flowers for special occasions. No extra romantic touch is too much trouble, from a hand-written French love poem or some hand picked music in an atmosphere that exudes pure, natural romance. Share a massage-for-two under the stars or in the privacy of your suite, or enjoy a sumptuous picnic of local cheeses, charcuterie, crusty breads and wine in a beautiful, secluded spot that boasts 360-degree views. In winter, snuggle up on comfy sofas to the crackling glow of a wood fire or delight in personalized wine tastings in the cosy cellar wine bar.

Browse through the hotel's generous stock of good books and enjoy the fine original art on the walls. Two very sociable dogs, one unsociable cat and seven hens provide plenty of background entertainment while a silky, chemical-free swimming pool is perfect for a romantic twilight dip. Help yourself to ripe tomatoes and plums from the garden or simply stay awhile, read, chat, sleep well and enjoy good food. When roses or oleander are in bloom you'll find a jugful in your room – together with a good bottle of Languedoc wine.

NICE

Loved by children the world over as a venue for adventurous play, tree-houses combine a touch of Tarzan with a lumberjack feel high up amongst the branches. Yet not every tree-perched wooden hut requires parental supervision – some are incredibly grown up, such as a collection of cosy, cedar-wood tree-houses between Cannes and Nice. Nestled amongst birds and squirrels, shielded by a mass of sprouting leaves, these most unusual tree-top retreats are big enough for adults and boast all the luxurious trappings of a fine hotel. You won't need a harness or jungle rope to access the wooden baths or open massage showers that peer out over branches – just a head for heights.

Owned by Diane Van den Berge, a Belgium national with an eco-green focus, the tree-houses are anything but basic, offering a gorgeous cedar-wood fragrance and high levels of comfort – not to mention Wi-Fi. After deciding that stone-built expansion would blight the landscape at her woodland plot, den Berge opted for a tree-house design for her B&B project. At five metres (16.5 ft)

off the ground, the largest house is 40 sq metres (430 sq ft) with a scenic terrace. Each is named after characters from *The Jungle Book* with guests that range from weekending couples on a romantic getaway to stressed-out urbanites keen to unwind.

Located on the flank of a valley, on the edge of a protected woodland zone, the Orion B&B is blessed with breathtaking views across untamed forest and the village of Saint-Paul de Vence. Extraordinary peace prevails, free from urban noise or light pollution where secluded relaxation areas offer a choice of sun or shade amidst oaks, pines, olive and palms. With the sweet sounds of nature the only distraction, the Orion claims to foster not only wellbeing, but also, simply 'being' – and rightly so. A chlorine-free, pebble-bottomed swimming pool self-cleans and requires no chemicals due to a sophisticated natural system of gravel and aquatic plant filtration that emulates an Alpine lake. Despite being scattered with dragon flies and forest flora the water remains gin-clear and refreshingly cool.

CONTACT
Orion B&B
Tel: +33 6 75 45 18 64
www.orionbb.com

Open from Easter until 30 December.
Prices start from 180 euros for two
people including breakfast.

*Hide out together in a
treehouse, complete with
picture-perfect treetop views.*

ITALY

TIME DIFFERENCE GMT +1

TELEPHONE CODE +39

CURRENCY Euro

LANGUAGE Italian

POPULATION 58.1 million

SIZE OF COUNTRY 301,336 sq km
(117,521 sq miles)

CAPITAL Rome

WHEN TO GO Italy's temperate climate has
regional variations but summers are warm and
sunny throughout. Humidity stifles the interior
region in summer, while winter tends to be cold,
damp and foggy. The ski season runs between
December and April and the best time to walk in
the Alps is between June and September, when
coastal Italy's warm waters are at their peak.

TOURIST INFORMATION
Italian Tourist Board
Tel: 020 7408 1254
Fax: 020 7399 3567
Email: italy@italiantouristboard.co.uk
www.italiantouristboard.co.uk

Europe's stylish boot-shaped peninsula dips its toe into the
Mediterranean Sea with two large islands, lava-rich Sicily and
Sardinia, part of its territory. The independent city-states of San
Marino and the Vatican City are also Italian. To the north, the Alps
separate Italy from France, Switzerland, Austria and Slovenia; to the
east, the River Po flows into the Adriatic Sea, while central Italy's
diverse Tuscan landscape contains snow-capped peaks, sloping
hills, sandy beaches and offshore islands. Hilly, broad grasslands
lead to vineyards, olive groves and pine forests, with Puglia, the 'heel
of the boot', wild, volcanic, isolated and marshy. Rome, Italy's capital
and largest city, boasts a stunning array of temple ruins, ornate
frescos and marble columns amidst noisy traffic, tooting horns and
pealing bells. Italy is also home to 41 UNESCO World Heritage Sites,
more than any other country on the planet.

CONTACTS
Emilia Romagna Turismo
Email: emiliaromagnaturismo
@regione.emilia-romagna.it
www.emiliaromagnaturismo.it

A 'bicycle made for two' is the perfect way to explore Emilia-Romagna's rolling countryside.

BOLOGNA

Weekending romantics who share a passion for cycling will discover that Italy's love for bicycles is quite unlike any other county in the world. Cycle-friendly Italy enjoys a long-standing love affair with human-powered, two-wheeled endeavour and offers an unmatched cycling terrain. Journey through vine-cloaked flats and rolling green hills to castle-topped climbing slopes on a thrilling terrain blessed with scenic beauty and some of the finest cuisine on the planet. Roads are also refreshingly free of congestion away from the cities with smooth-paved routes devoid of potholes and bumps. Numerous tour companies run cycling tours across the region. Many offer a choice of itineraries from a gentle plod around country lanes to a full-on Giro d'Italia-style assault. Having a suggested route to follow takes a lot of the pre-planning out of the weekend – simply pump up the tyres, unfurl the map and go. Fed up with travelling 50 yards behind your partner? Then opt for a tandem, cycling's unbeatable machine-for-two. Next, enjoy shared views and asphalt-pounding synchronicity in Italy; a nation where cycling is worshipped like a religion and bicycles are always welcome.

Named after Via Emilia, the old Roman road linking Rimini to Piacenza, Emilia-Romagna stretches from the Adriatic Sea to the wide, open plains of Italy's north to form a ragged kite-shaped expanse. Covering fishing villages, salt pans and medieval towns, past rolling hills, spire, towers and abbeys, Emilia-Romagna is renowned for many of Italy's most celebrated exports, such Prosciutto di Parma, Tortellini, Lasagna, Parmigiano Reggiano, Ferrari and Ducati. The region is also awash with colour – leafy landscapes ensure a heady scenic blur as one pretty village blends into another and the miles slip effortlessly by.

Companionship is the appeal of riding a tandem. Couples can communicate easily with each other with no need to wobble close enough to hear or yell. A tandem has the same wind resistance as a single bike in the exhilarating, rushing wind, allowing down-hill high speeds together. On a bicycle made for two', experiences are collective with united challenges and views. Riding a tandem builds mutual trust and enables a couple to share the workload, especially uphill. In turn, Emilia-Romagna is renowned for its friendliness and hospitality and nothing brings out the region's generosity quite like a romantic couple on a tandem, so be sure to leave time for a pit stop at a wine-stall at the side of the road in order to raise a glass 'to the road'.

ROME

CONTACTS
Happy Rent
Tel: +39 6 42 02 06 75
Email: hri@happyrent.com
www.happyrent.com

For a list of Rome's scooter and
vespa hire companies:
www.tassoni.it/guide/
moto-bike-rent.htm

Rome Tourism
Tel: +39 6 48 89 91
www.romeinfo.com

*Rome's legendary sights call
for classic charm with just
a dash of the carefree.*

Gregory Peck and Audrey Hepburn epitomise stylish chic in the giddily romantic *Roman Holiday*: a magical 1950s romantic comedy that highlights the anarchic joys of a couple in love. Flirty misunderstandings, jealous distrust and disapproval provide heavy romantic undertones, with the handsome streets of ancient Rome the perfect backdrop for a gripping romance.

Peck's portrayal of a darkly handsome but cynical American newshound is perfectly complimented by Hepburn's role as the elfin-faced, pampered European princess. Curious twists to the plot – as mysterious as Rome's cobbled labyrinthine streets – throw the couple together, neither knowing much about the other. A scene-stealing sequence of Hepburn riding off side-saddle on Peck's Vespa secured iconic brand status to all involved – Rome, the film, the actors and the impossibly cool Vespa. Peck ends up on the seat behind Hepburn, clinging to her as she screeches around Rome, scattering pedestrians and careering the wrong way down one-way streets. Not since the olden days of tandems had a two-person mode of transport so perfectly captured romantic chic, inspiring millions of love-birds, from Salvador Dali to Jennifer Lopez, to snap one up for their own cosy sojourns. Beautifully simple, sturdy, economical and ingeniously designed to keep the clothes of the rider spotlessly clean, the Vespa has it all, including an engine that sounds like a mosquito that is undoubtedly part of its charm. Automatic transmission and a three-speed gear change ensure a top speed of 50 km per hour allowing couples to nip, Roman Holiday-style, around the Italian capital with true panache. Tourists can now relive the romance by hiring a vintage Vespa.

Couples that decide to forgo Rome's cutesy horse-drawn carriages in favour of an altogether different nostalgic elegance will find a vintage Vespa perfectly primed for a romantic jaunt. A spacious bench-seat offers ample room for a cuddle during a break mid-journey – as depicted in Vespa's 2002 ad campaign, 'The Sexiest Way to Get from A-B'. It is also faultlessly sized to accommodate a standard picnic hamper (once his-and-hers helmets have been removed). An unexpected level of respect is afforded by Rome's speed-crazed car drivers to the sight of a couple entwined on an elderly scooter. So, not only do they weave through traffic, fit into tight parking spaces and offer an excuse to clutch the object of your affections, they also melt the heart of every Italian racer who has ever seen Hepburn or Peck.

A simple push-button start ensures even first-timers can get to grip with a Vespa without the need to consult a manual or break into a sweat. Another reassuring prospect is the Vespa's steadfast reliability record: mechanical mishaps are, thankfully, a rarity even when the scooter is charmingly vintage. Fuel consumption, however, remains a mystery despite an impressive gauge. If spluttering unexpectedly to halt threatens to impact on the romance of your Roman foray, be sure to top up after tearing around.

For the romantic in Rome, Vespas allow the blissful freedom to weave along alleyways normally off-limits to vehicles. Scoot away from the city's madcap junctions to discover quiet, flower-filled plazas and sprinkling fountains. Head down cobblestone streets at whim to explore merchants and artisans unseen by the city's tourist hordes. Then whiz around Piazza Della Republica before zipping by the Piazza Santa Maria Maggiore to Via Merulana and heading to the Piazza San Giovanni for a bowl of *Nutella Gelato* – a gooey, chocolate-and-nut ice cream, ordered to share. Pluck a rose from a flower stall at pretty Via Santissimi Quattro before speeding around the Colosseum and Arch of the Constantine ahead of a full-throttle burst into the Parco Del Celio to listen to the beautifully romantic strains of gypsy violins. At the Testaccio, enjoy views of the grand Monte dei Cocci before scooting along picturesuqe Lungotevere Aventino to the Isola Tiberina to share a slice of pizza and a kiss by the so-called Lover's Wall. Then weave through the crowds along Via Garibaldi and Piazza Venezia to the palacial grandeur of the Via Del Quirinale where the prancing horses of the obilisque denote the perfect spot for a self-timed photograph to capture the romance of the trip – and Rome itself.

CONTACTS
Orient Express
Tel: +44 (0)845 077 2222
www.orient-express.com

Venetian Tourist Board
Tel: +39 4 15 29 87 11
Email: info@turismovenezia.it
www.turismovenezia.it

*Take in the glorious scenery
from the window of your
compartment before a dawn
arrival in Paris.*

VENICE

Few train journeys can conjure up the same intrigue and opulence as travelling aboard the legendary Orient Express. For over 100 years the world's most glamorous train has epitomized romance, mystery and extravagance, providing a luxurious carriage to wealthy widows, royalty, masters of espionage and at least a couple of assassins. Today, it continues to evoke intrigue and allure as the inspiration behind six major films, 19 books and a fox trot, choreographed in 1933. Romantic and unashamedly regal, few modes of transport can claim such exemplary service or bygone sophistication as this fabled string of Pullmans. Climb aboard to follow the route of an Agatha Christie novel or James Bond thriller on the undisputed King of Trains – where first-class travel is guaranteed.

The original route of the Orient Express, in 1883, was from Paris to Giurgiu in Romania via Munich and Vienna. The year 1889 saw the completion of a direct rail line to Istanbul. After surviving World War II, the Orient Express underwent numerous modifications before grinding to a dilapidated halt in 1977. Saved by entrepreneur and rail enthusiast James B.

Sherwood, who snapped up the train's carriages at a Sotheby's auction in Monte Carlo, the Orient Express was lavished with a US $16 million overhaul of 35 of its vintage sleepers, Pullmans and restaurant cars. On 25th May 1982 the legend was reborn when the Venice Simplon-Orient-Express made its maiden journey from London to Venice. Unlike the Graeme Greene novel suggests, there have been several Orient Express trains, some of which have been famously bombed, shot at and perilously marooned.

Today, the gleaming livery of the Venice Simplon-Orient-Express traverses Europe on one of the most romantic journeys in the world. Each beautifully restored 1920s and '30s carriage boasts a history of its own after long years of service criss-crossing European frontiers. A grand, ornate bastion of nostalgic elegance in a modern world, the Pullman remains one of the greatest innovations of the 19th century in terms of transport technology and opulence. Hand-crafted, polished wood, Lalique glass, sweeping drapes, chandeliers and brass fittings set the tone in this most luxurious moving hotel. Sleeping Car 3425 was a part of the Orient-Express service used by

King Carol of Romania, whilst keen railway enthusiast King Boris III of Bulgaria is rumoured to have taken the footplate to drive the train himself. Sleeping Car 3309 was part of the 1929 service that was stuck in a snow drift for ten days, 97 km (60 miles) outside Istanbul. Other carriages saw active service during World War II either at the hands of the US Transportation Corps or the German Army – but never incognito.

From the moment a passenger boards at Venice, immaculately dressed staff in spotless uniforms cater to their every whim, be it champagne in the 1920's-style piano bar or a multi-course gourmet dinner in a choice of two fine restaurants. With trays poised and smiles at the ready, the service excels at every level to ensure each wide-eyed guest enjoys the romantic ride of their lives. Nothing is too much trouble, simply push a little button and ask for anything you desire. People celebrate honeymoons, anniversaries and all manner of major milestones aboard the Orient Express, from an important birthday to finding their mate for life. Settle into an upholstered couch to marvel at an ever-changing landscape of snow-covered mountains, flower-filled meadows, Alpine chalets and grand villas whilst being thoroughly spoiled. A trio of carriages containing the bar and restaurants offer distinctly individual décor and character, from etched Art Deco glass to mahogany pieces inlaid with black lacquer chinoiserie and marquetry. Tables groan under the weight of French crystal and Italian linen, while menus read like a Who's Who of fine wine-growers and fresh produce from Continental Europe and beyond.

Cosy compartments offer adequate room for a one-night, two-day sojourn. They are also where the Orient Express's famous afternoon tea is served. A delicate rap at the door signifies the arrival of the steward armed with a tray of fine china, Earl Grey tea and delectable little pastries. Curl up with a book to enjoy the passing scenery as preparations for a grand dinner commence. 'You cannot be overdressed' states the Orient Express brochure – and never was a truer word spoken. Crimson silks, white tuxedos, kilts with velvet coat and tails in baronial hues, with women of all ages swathed in sparkling jewels and decorated with fans and feather boas. First, a toast: to life and love, over a champagne aperitif. Next, a memorable, four-course feast amidst a dazzling display of beautifully presented dishes delivered with theatrical aplomb. Highlights include crab and smoked salmon parcels followed by tender tournedos of beef with white truffle butter, and fresh vanilla ice cream with pistachio pralines.

As the last diners sip their night-caps to the gentle sound of tinkling ivories, each Orient Express compartment is transformed into a bedroom suite, complete with monogrammed Egyptian cotton sheets. Then, voila! A Parisian vista welcomes passengers the next morning as the train winds its way up through French vineyards and fruit orchards. Sip roasted coffee as this most romantic voyage unfurls in an unending ripple of exquisite style. Next stop, London – after another glass of champagne, of course.

'Overdressed' is not part of the language aboard this most romantic of trains.

030

FLORENCE

CONTACTS
Villa San Michele
Tel: +39 5 55 67 82 00
Fax: +39 5 55 67 82 50
Email: info@villasanmichele.net
www.villasanmichele.com

Cavolo Nero
Tel: +39 5 52 94 744
www.cavolonero.it

I Renailo
Tel: +39 3 47 79 82 356
Email: info@renaiolo.it
www.renaoilo.it

Caffe Concerto
Tel: +39 5 56 77 377
Fax: +39 5 56 76 493
www.caffeconcerto.net

*The beautiful River Arno, with
its rhythmic punctuation
of bridges.*

Discovering romantic Florence (Firenze) can be as easy as simply throwing open your windows to frame the view. Few cities in the world boast such an awe-inspiring rooftop panorama, encapsulating a muddle of terracotta tiles, clock towers and caramel-coloured spires against a crowded backdrop of rolling green hills. Merely being in the midst of Florence's heart-stopping architectural splendour can produce a sensory overload, such is the city's colour, grandeur and imposing presence. Head to the Piazza della Signoria to start the day with a frothy cappuccino before yielding to the lure of the palatial Uffizi Gallery's collection of Renaissance art (pre-book to avoid a 4-hour queue).

Next, hop aboard the courtesy bus, outside department store La Rinascente on Piazza della Repubblica, for uber-swish Villa San Michele and a decadent lunch with to-die-for views. Once a Franciscan monastery, luxurious Villa San Michele is today one of Europe's most exclusive Renaissance villas, with a façade attributed to Michelangelo. A gorgeous 17th-century stone-built loggia affords unforgettable vistas across Fiesole and the city of Florence; a Tuscan lunch and dinner menu (from 30 Euros) is also served here.

Hotel guests enjoy first-class service, with no expense spared, amidst rolling countryside dotted with fragrant blooms, yet close to the art treasures of Florence. Expect Egyptian cotton sheets, rose petals, perfumed candles, and soaps produced by the famous Farmacia di Santa Maria Novella, plus an illustrated book on Florence.

Tuscany's magnificent cultural and arts hub sits on the banks of the expansive River Arno, between the Adriatic and the Tyrrhenian seas, in the midst of the Italian peninsula. Boasting exceptional artistic patrimony that remains a glorious testimony to the city's rich history, every part of Florence appears rich in stucco swirls and grandiose flurries. Spectacular art abounds, be it in the city's streets or behind the doors of world-renowned museums, from elegant sculptures to works by globally revered grand masters. Hand-holding couples stroll across bird-scattered piazzas once frequented by Cimabue and Giotto,

the fathers of Italian painting. Thanks to Dante, Florence is also the city in which the Italian language was born – a melodic linguistic style envied by would-be Casanovas worldwide. Today, Florence remains an epicentre of intense cultural and literary activity at the heart of European classical art history. To visit is to become immersed in an eye-popping array of Renaissance beauty, from Brunelleschi's most resplendent dome to the romantic charms of Botticelli's Venus.

Back in the heart of the city, marvel at the Galleria dell'Accademia, where Michelangelo's David, the world's best-known hunk of marble, is the major draw. Next, meander across the Ponte Vecchio, an ancient bridge straddling the Arno's girth, on which lovers still 'lock their love' by placing a padlock on the railings and tossing keys into the water as a sign of their commitment to each other; this romantic declaration dates backs generation in Florence, though the gesture is now discouraged by a hefty 2,000 Euro fine.

As the afternoon sunlight fades from the hills, take a taxi to the green-and-white marble San Miniato al Monte above the city, a handsome Romanesque church where the resident Benedictines sing Gregorian chants during late-afternoon vespers at 5pm each day. From the echoing cloisters, the monks' soaring tones emanate through the chambers to create a glorious ethereal ambience. Afterwards, follow the stone steps down into San Frediano, Florence's old quarter, to enjoy an aperitif at cosy Cavaolo Nero on Via d'Ardiglione, before meeting Paolo Bruni for a *renaiolo* trip along the River Arno. Using a single, skinny 8-metre oar to plough through the waters from a standing stance, a sweeping motion pushes the boats along much like a Venetian gondolier. Snuggle beneath blankets under a moonlit sky to experience Florence at a leisurely pace, passing biscuit-coloured buildings adorned with flower-filled cast-iron balconies and flickering lamps, before alighting for a fine dinner at charming Caffe Concerto. Pick a table overlooking the riverbanks to hide amongst exotic pot plants and eclectic antiques whilst relishing delectable *crêpes al limone* to the soft sounds of jazz.

031

TODI

CONTACTS
Perugia Tourism Office
Tel: +39 7 55 73 64 58
http://tourism.comune.perugia.it

Some say Todi's foliage-rich linden tree dates back to the 14th century which, if true, makes the town's 'Tree of Lovers' one of the oldest in the world. In folklore, the linden's heart-shaped leaves were dedicated to Venus, the goddess of love. In Todi, the tree evokes a romantic notion of centuries-old sentiment, from rekindled romances to marriage proposals and declarations of undying love. Dryads, or tree spirits, are said to be wedded to Linden trees, while in Roman mythology, the Linden tree is a symbol of conjugal love and fidelity. In times past, a leaf plucked from the linden tree symbolized the sanctity of life-long union. Today this tree provides a secluded enclave, allowing hand-entwined couples to drink in the romance of Todi's romantic history.

Few cities are bestowed such a rich legacy of Medieval and Renaissance art as Todi, a historic settlement of stunning Gothic grandeur, blessed with flawless piazzas and trapezoidal towers. Set on a beautiful Umbrian hilltop, surrounded by undulating, sunflower-filled meadows, Todi's rich array of Etruscan bronzes, Roman monuments, sculptures, spires, frescoes and arches is one of Italy's most authentic – and most striking. Much is unchanged, from the majesty of the architecture to the ancient fields tended by families who have tilled the soil and looked after their vineyards and olive groves for generations. Then there is the linden tree, strong and untroubled for 700 years or more, still emitting its haunting fragrance and dripping with thick, sweet honeydew.

Stroll Todi's outdoor gallery of Romanesque, medieval and Gothic splendour to discover churches, bell towers and ornate facades in a meandering warren of cobbled streets spilling down hilly slopes. Enjoy an *aperitivo* or cappuccino in the palace-hemmed Piazza del Popolo to be transported back to the Middle Ages amidst travertine stone walls, vast cathedrals, storied frescoes and gilded treasures. Under the watchful gaze of the ancient Church of San Fortunato, feast on a veritable medieval banquet of fine art and antiques before seeking out the linden tree – Todi's much-fabled bastion of romance.

Explore Todi's winding, storied streets together as dusk falls.

MILAN

The language of flowers and their symbolic sentiments have been immortalised by the pen of a thousand poets across time. From Oscar Wilde's apologetic *Flower of Love* and *Perfect Flower* by wordsmith David Morris to the evocative *My Flower* by Sidney Frances, a symbiotic tale of velvety petals and romance, flowers represent one of the oldest means to express affection, love, gratitude and a host of other emotions. They convey a thought in time, and imply intention, affection and appreciation.

Mood-moderating floral fragrance can bring about feelings of joy, tranquillity and happiness as the nerve endings in our olfactory system deliver powerful sensory messages from the nose to the brain. Flowers also have a strong positive effect on our emotional wellbeing and are a natural aphrodisiac for passionate response, from the rose's connotations of love and beauty to the camellia's message of longing. Consider too the lasting affection expressed by the delicate forget-me-not or a daisy's pledge of loyalty, a daffodil's unrequited love, the secret passion of the gardenia and the eternal love and fidelity assured by sweet-smelling orange blossom.

On a single Monday in April, Milan surrenders to the intensity of floral splendour in a 400-year-old Franciscan tradition in which thousands of varicoloured blooms take centre stage. Covering every pavestone on the charming Piazza Sant'Angelo, the Lunedì dell'Angelo's flower market was the brainchild of the ancient monastery of St Angelo and its green-fingered brethren. Bunches of fluted, tall-stemmed daisies on a floral carpet of fluffy begonias provide a fragrant riot of colour together with vast buckets of hibiscuses, lilies and slender-necked roses. Blooms of fuchsia pink and vibrant crimson vie for position amongst petals of deep purple, white, yellow and orange, fanned by a heady, perfumed breeze.

Linked with devotion in Italian folklore, on account of its attentive, nodding head that follows the sun across the sky, the sunflower enjoys pride of place, adding bright golden splashes across the plaza. Sweethearts, however, hover starry-eyed around stalls of red camellia, whose delicate feather-headed blooms carry a strong romantic subtext: 'you're a flame in my heart'.

CONTACTS
Milan Tourist Office
Piazza del Duomo 19/A
Tel: +39 2 77 40 43 43
www.provincia.milano.it

April brings a riot of colour to Milan's streets.

CONTACTS
Turismo de Pisa
Tel: +39 5 09 29 777
Fax: +39 5 09 29 764
Email: aptpisa@pisaturismo.it
www.pisaturismo.it

Tours run daily, from 5 euros
per person.

*Pisa's broad waterway offers
the possibility of a romantic
sightseeing voyage.*

PISA

Pisa's famous leaning tower boasts a keenly observed romantic legend pertaining to lovers who visit to climb the 294 stone steps together. Built in 1173, Italy's iconic *campanile* (bell tower) boasts a well-worn, uneven, slippery ascent, trodden millions of times over many centuries. Pisa's romantic legend dictates that for a life-long, happy union, a couple should make a wish at the top of tower. Many do so; with hands entwined, romantic hopes and dreams are shared as they drink in the jaw-dropping vistas across the city at a height of almost 56 metres.

A broad waterway that neatly divides Pisa before flowing into the Tyrrhenian Sea, the mighty River Arno forms the spiritual backbone of city. Today, unlike maritime eras past, the coast is 12 km (7 miles) away, a result of shifting river silt congesting the watercourse downstream. Yet Pisa and seamanship remain inextricably linked by a centuries-old tradition of dockyards and shipbuilding. In the Early Middle Ages, Pisa was a lively trading port and one of Italy's four Maritime Republics (the other three were Genoa, Venice and Amalfi). Today, this seafaring heritage is celebrated each year during a colourful regatta season, culminating in the *Regata delle Repubbliche* Marinare in June. Traversing the city's silvery watercourse offers a romantic sightseeing voyage through Pisa's storied maritime past steeped in nautical tales of Greek sailing vessels and the legend of Pelops. Glide past grand, stucco mansions, paved palazzos, Neo-classical churches and old clock-towers to the leafy, green park of San Rossore at the estuary with the Tyrrhenian Sea. Dine on succulent seafood spaghetti in the picturesque Marina di Pisa whilst gazing out across stunning waters rich in nautical legend and seafaring romance.

Pisa boasts innumerable romantic connotations but is best known for its association with British romantic poet Percy Bysshe Shelley (1792–1822) who composed the great body of his work in Italy, moving to Pisa in 1820. Blatantly personal *Epipsychidion* (1821) owes its heartfelt sentiment to Emilia Viviani, a young woman that Shelley met in Pisa and with whom he developed a brief but intense union. Shelley's lyrical belief in the power of human love superbly masters the beauty, grandeur and romance of the city, writing: 'Into the height of Love's rare Universe, are chains of lead around its flight of fire - I pant, I sink, I tremble, I expire!'.

SARDINIA

Writer and boating enthusiast Herb Payson summed up the riches of life on the water with the rhetorical: 'Who can feel poor when the sails are full and the spirit is full?'. Certainly, on Sardinia's dazzling waters vast riches are abundantly evident, from the gleaming 100-ft yachts with six-figure price-tags to the tanned, barefoot champions of leisure enjoying the shoreline high life on Millionaire's Row. Yet sailing this spectacular coastline between Italy, Spain and Tunisia isn't solely for the top-earners of the Forbes 500; Sardinia's treasures are easily accessible without the glitz and glamour. Charming and humble at heart, and blessed by an irrepressible air of romantic nostalgia, to explore Sardinia by boat is to discover its heart, according to locals.

Couples seeking waterborne seclusion are spoilt for choice in Sardinia, where sailing offers innumerable options for novices and experienced boaters alike. Dozens of yacht charters to suit every budget, style and character offer cruises around the island's emerald waters. Many delve into some of the hundreds of secluded coves and picture-book beaches whilst skirting the dramatic rock formations that characterize Sardinia's rugged coast. Experienced sailors have access to world-class marinas that offer nautical maps and directories free of charge. A big pull for sailors is the coastline's diversity, from the rounded dunes of the Costa Verde to the deep emerald coves and ragged cliffs of Cala Gonone. No stretch of shoreline is the same – a major draw with the moneyed and much-travelled boating crowd – yet Sardinia's simple fishing roots ensure the island remains low-key and unpretentious. A laid-back vibe prevails across the island, even when yet another A-list name weighs anchor and steps ashore.

English skipper Tim Carrington runs romantic charters aboard *Lady H*, his 36-ft cruiser, from Il Porto Marina in the harbour of Santa Teresa on Sardinia's northern tip. Sardinia enjoys a long tradition as a destination for honeymooners and romantic couples, offering plenty of beautiful, secluded spots in which to picnic, swim and soak up unspoilt scenic views. Dive into translucent blue seas to experience a kaleidoscope of underwater colours or stroll along smooth white-sand beaches dotted with hidden coves. Trips can be wholly tailored to suit the occasion, from flower-filled Valentine's Day surprises to sunset proposals on the waves.

CONTACTS
Just Sardinia
Tel: +44 (0)1202 484 858
Email: holidays@justsardinia.co.uk
www.justsardinia.co.uk

Sardinia Tourism
Email: sardegnaturismo@
regione.sardegna.it
www.sardegnaturismo.it

Under a sapphire-blue sky, find waterborne seclusion on Sardinia's dazzling turquoise waters.

035

SICILY

GETTING THERE
Atelier Sul Mare is a one-hour
transfer from Palermo, or two hours
from either Catania or Messina

CONTACTS
Atelier Sul Mare (Art Hotel)
Tel:+39 9 21 33 42 91
Email: info@ateliersulmare.it
www.ateliersulmare.it

Francesco Fontana
Tel: +39 3 38 13 28 003
Email: info@francescofontana.com
www.francescofontana.com

*Find mellow seclusion inside
before enjoying spectacular
views out to sea.*

Sicilian art history follows a rich trail of civilisations and cultures, from ancient Phoenicians and Greeks to Romans, Arabs, Saracens, Normans and Spanish. Each has left a vibrant and indelible mark on the island's diverse artistic make-up, a legacy that touches the spirit of Sicilians in a myriad of genres and traditions. At the centre of the Mediterranean Sea, Sicily has played a pivotal role in Mediterranean history for over 3,000 years. Important artistic, architectural, and cultural remains are visible at virtually every town in almost every corner of the island. Grand temples, rugged mountains, grassy plains and a wave-lashed coastline are evocatively captured in oils, pastels and pencil drawings together with the mythological and volcanic Aeolian Islands. On the Phoenician island of Mozia, sweeping saltpans lie dotted with red-capped windmills; Norman towns sit perched atop ancient burial sites partially bordered by the sea; old, deep moats and fortified towers have yielded many ancient treasures of water-filled caves and Roman ruins sprinkled with mosaics in every hue. Mementoes of a sacred Greek heritage lead to aristocratic villas, rustic farms and beige-coloured, pebbled beaches; centuries-old olive groves sit amongst yellow fields, palm trees and tumbling vines. Amongst all of this, top-quality wines, exported around the world, and fresh local food form the core of a deep-rooted cooking tradition offer a visual and gastronomic feast that ensures Sicily remains a paradise isle.

In the fine arts, Sicily's contribution has been enormous, from the works of Antonello di Messina

to Renato Guttuso. Today, Sicily celebrates its artistic passion in a diverse assortment of galleries and festivals and is also home to the Atelier Sul Mare, Italy's only contemporary art hotel. Housed in a Mediterranean-style building that doubles as a contemporary art gallery, the hotel overlooks the seafront in the charming Sicilian fishing village of Castel di Tusa. Although the name doesn't neatly translate into English, it loosely means something like 'artist's studio by the sea' – an accurate description. Original artworks adorn every available space, inside and out, while flower-decked terraces enjoy jaw-dropping views out to sea. Fifteen resident artists in turn have spent time in this unconventional hotel, resulting in rooms that are installation pieces – a traditional seaside hotel this is not. Only a few rooms border on the way-too-garish so if you are risk-averse ask for one of the calmer seascapes over the Avant Garde or Surrilest suites. Couples do sacrifice a degree of comfort in the name of art, but are entertaining nonetheless, thanks to cutting-edge conceptual design with whitewashed curves and irregular windows. No two rooms are even remotely the same, which makes for an unforgettable stay.

Each of the Atelier Sul Mare's individually designed Art Bedrooms are hung with paintings by artists Danielle Mitterand, Agnese Purgatorio, Antonio Presti, Renato Curcio Luigi Michele Vincenzo Consolo and Umberto Leone e Ute Pyka. This is a revolutionary project to shake up perceptions of hotel art, so guests at Atelier sul Mare aren't considered mere passive observers but rather essential protagonists of the artistic experience itself. An authentic Sicilian eatery serves as a gallery for itinerant collections allowing guests to dine whilst soaking up the artistic essence of this inspiring land.

Fancy immortalising your arty stay with a commissioned portrait? Then contact Sicilian artist Francesco Fontana for a lasting artistic memento of your romantic Sicilian visit. An acclaimed oil and watercolour painter, Fontana has exhibited in France and Italy. His bold representations capture personality, mood and even romantic affection with deft brushstrokes that beautifully engage the subject with the viewer. The Atelier Sul Mare's owner Signor Presti has a contacts book that reads like a Who's Who of the Sicilian art world from charcoal aficionados skilled at sketching a romantic pose to abstract painters keen to apply their own unique perspective. But perhaps the most exciting art project at the Atelier Sul Mare is the individual imprint each guest can leave. Add, interact, contemplate and inwardly digest the decor before responding with your own personal touch, be it a daub, a splash or collage. Couples can choose from the strong red of *Power* (Maurizio Marchetti), the passionate red and white of the *Absorbing Nest* (Paolo Icaro) or the minimalist *Mystery for the Moon* (Hidetoshi Nagasawa). Each is a masterpiece, so be sure to leave something more imaginative than: Me 4 You S.W.A.L.K xxx.

No two rooms in this inspirational hotel are remotely the same.

SWITZERLAND

TIME DIFFERENCE GMT +1

TELEPHONE CODE +41

CURRENCY Swiss Franc

LANGUAGE Schwitzerdütsch (Swiss German),
French, Italian and Romansh

POPULATION 7.5 million

SIZE OF COUNTRY 41,295 sq km
(16,105 sq miles)

CAPITAL Bern

WHEN TO GO Although renowned for its
snowy, cold ski regions, Switzerland is blessed
with over 290 days of sunshine and boasts
warm summers when temperatures can rise
to around 30°C (86°F). Even in the mountains
the sun is hot, while winters rarely become
cold enough to drop below -5°C (23°F), apart
from on higher ground.

TOURIST INFORMATION
Swiss National Tourist Office
Tel: +41 800 100 200 30
Fax: +41 800 100 200 31
Email: info.uk@myswitzerland.com
www.myswitzerland.com

Lying east of France and north of Italy, Switzerland is primarily a
mountainous landscape with the rising peaks of the Alps in the south
and the Jura in the northwest. A grassy central plateau of rolling hills,
plains and large lakes forms the heart of this sophisticated Alpine
nation amidst sparkling, snow-covered downhill ski slopes and cross
country trails. In summer, these white-topped peaks are transformed
into wildflower meadows and scenic picnic spots while the cities of
Geneva, Zurich and Bern, edged with rivers, lakes and leafy paths,
offer an array of shopping and fine dining.

CONTACTS
Verbier Limited Edition
Tel: 0800 716919
www.thelodge.virgin.com

Geneva Tourist Office
Tel: +41 (0)22 909 70 00
Fax +41 (0)22 909 70 11
www.geneve-tourisme.ch

*Treat a loved-one to the cosiest
of luxury getaways in Verbier's
most decadent lodge.*

GENEVA

Richard Branson describes his über-luxurious chalet as 'Necker in the snow', referring to the exclusive Caribbean paradise islet he famously lets out to a star-studded millionaire crowd. Since it opened in 2007, Branson's top-notch chalet has become suitably fashionable with a super-chic clientele. Like Necker Island, The Lodge, Verbier, guarantees its guests total privacy and anonymity and, following a £3.5-million refurbishment, can also be trusted to deliver on style and service. It's not cheap, of course, but the Lodge does boast an exceptional location on the near-perfect ski slopes in the snow-encrusted Valais. During their stay, the Lodge is a home-from-home with lavish furnishings and top-of-the-range technology that includes a plasma TV the size of a double-decker bus. Together with an indoor pool and mini ice rink there is an indoor and outdoor Jacuzzi and fully equipped gymnasium. Guests also have their own driver on call, 24 hours a day (within Verbier), and are encouraged to help themselves to food and free-flowing Champagne.

Although the Lodge's alpine chic is wholly different to Branson's swish Caribbean getaway, the similarities with the gorgeous, larch-wood lodge lie in the fact that it appeals to the same glitzy set. An impeccably appointed interior reworks the traditional Alpine style with chalky, textured buttermilk and earth tones. Rug-scattered reclaimed oak floors and a 20-seater sofa dominate the lounge area where the Bransons' family photos take pride of place on the shelves. Every room has a Bose digital radio, iPod dock, enormous bottles of Cowshed toiletries, fluffy robes and egg-shaped baths – complete with designer rubber ducks.

So, back to the subject of prices: is the Lodge really so eye-wateringly expensive? Well yes, and no. Given that pretty much everything is included in the tariff, be it Champagne on tap, most meals, ski guides or spa treatments, the £42,300 winter starting price for exclusive use (for 18 guests) begins to look (almost) modest for a one-week stay. However, it is the 3-night summer breaks that are luring romantic couples to this swankiest of wooden chalets. Over 400 km (248 miles) of wild-flower trails offer excellent walking in rugged countryside. A Jacuzzi the size of the Serpentine and thirteen staff at your beck and call (including a chef who worked with Raymond Blanc), ensure the Lodge is perfect for a romantic sojourn, from £11,590 for a double room.

037

CONTACTS
Hotel Uto Kulm
Tel. +41 (0) 44 457 66 66
Fax +41 (0) 44 457 66 99
Email: info@utokulm.ch
www.utokulm.ch

Zurich Tourist Office
Tel. +41 44 215 40 00
Fax +41 44 215 40 80
Email: information@zuerich.com
www.zuerich.com

Let romance go sky-high at the top of Zurich.

ZURICH

For decades, Zurich's highest hotel has charmed guests with its tucked-away location, close to the city yet seemingly in another world. Set on an unspoilt hillside, in lush greenery untroubled by traffic, the Hotel Uto Kulm enjoys blessed panoramas 'at the top of Zurich'.

Of the hotel's 55 rooms, nine individual suites are wholly dedicated to *amour* with a minimalist, smooch-worthy decor refreshingly free from rapturous hearts-and-flowers. Unashamedly created for couples keen to share heartfelt soirees, the Uto Kulm's romantic suites have each been stylishly furnished and are the epitome of contemporary chic. Each boasts a unique focal point, be it a retro-styled cuddling couch with stunning views amongst candyfloss clouds or a whirlpool for two. Others are equipped with wood-burning stoves and Champagne on ice. Heart-shaped hot tubs with moonlight views frame a neon-lit Zurich skyline and star-studded sky. A Bang & Olufsen sound system ensures the mood is heightened by hand-picked ballads while you make exclusive use of the sauna and spa.

Accessible by train or on foot, with porters that transport luggage up the hill, the hotel is quite unlike any other in Zurich. Expansive swathes of Alpine foliage hem the Uto Klum in all directions from sunny, flower-filled scrub to snow-dusted pines. Against a backdrop of white-topped mountains, from the Uetliberg out across the city, the Uto Kulm's ever-changing vistas offer some of the finest twilight skies in Switzerland, with colours running from softest pink to inky purple riddled with crimson.

Beneath this magical sunset, a short stroll through woodland leads you to a candlelit restaurant, or simply ask your butler to serve the award-winning Gourmand connoisseur menu in your suite: delicious 5-course lobster, oysters and shared Swiss fondue meal is sufficiently delectable to make anyone go weak at the knees.

Prices for the hotel's special tete-a-tete packages start at 200 Swiss Francs (CFH) per person for a Romantic suite, including Champagne, unlimited freshly brewed coffee, huge buffet breakfast, 95-minute spa treatment and gourmet dinner.

GSTAAD

Though distinctly less high-profile than its French namesake 400 km away, a road sign still warmly welcomes visitors to the charming Swiss village of Champagne. Lying on the dreamy vine-trimmed France-Switzerland border, the Swiss Champagne settlement was founded by 9th-century settlers. However, while the two Champagnes share a name – and a passion for wine – only the bigger French concern has the legal right to use it on their local produce. Contrary to a European Court ruling, Switzerland has yet to officially rename its sparkly stuff. So to avoid any infringement on the billion-dollar prestige of France's Champagne region, it is advisable to order in hushed tones, or point.

While Switzerland's Champagne doesn't boast the grapes or the provenance of its counterpart over the border, it does produce a perfectly quaffable array of wines. Before the EU ruling, Swiss vintners sold over 110,000 bottles of this light, delicate liquid. Villagers have been making wine for at least 800 years, producing around 280,000 bottles of its almost-bubbly variety in around 40 of its small, family-run wine-growing farms. Today, without the Champagne label, sales are down almost 70 percent. Yet, in true romantic David-and-Goliath style, the Swiss are fighting back as this small, friendly village of 700 people

attempts to put its Champagne on the map. With the help of wine stores and buyers across Switzerland, the wine of Switzerland's gnarled and knotty grape-clad slopes has raised its domestic profile. At around 5 Euros a bottle, the Swiss fizz lacks the finesse (and the price tag) of the more refined French tipple. Yet share a bottle on a warm, sunny day with a loved one and it is romance personified.

Synonymous with the Champagne-swilling, wealthy elite, the Swiss ski resort of Gstaad epitomizes the finest luxuries in life. As one of the more upmarket destinations to offer Swiss growers its backing, visitors can taste and purchase home-spun Champagne from a number of the town's finest wine purveyors. Visitors on a romantic sojourn can take advantage of a sumptuous weekend package at the city's Grand Hotel Bellevue. A two-night stay is captured for posterity by professional photographer Romel Janeski, including make-up and a 3-hour shoot. Breakfast in bed, gourmet tête-à-tête dinners and a luxurious Japanese bath for two illuminated by the soft glow of candles are just a few of the romantic touches. After a private late-night dip in the pool and a shared Jacuzzi, retire to your flower-decked luxury suite to enjoy chocolate-dipped strawberries and fine Champagne – Swiss or French.

CONTACTS
Grand Hotel Bellevue
Tel: +41 33 748 00 00
Fax +41 33 748 00 01
Email: info@bellevue-gstaad.ch
www.bellevue-gstaad.com

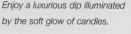

Enjoy a luxurious dip illuminated by the soft glow of candles.

LUXEMBOURG

TIME DIFFERENCE GMT +1

TELEPHONE CODE +352

CURRENCY Euro

LANGUAGES Luxembourgish, French and German

POPULATION 480,222

SIZE OF COUNTRY 2,568 sq km (1,002 sq miles)

CAPITAL Luxembourg City

WHEN TO GO Summers in Luxembourg can be warm, dry and sunny although showers remain common year-round. Northern regions are wetter, with June and September often the best months for hiking, climbing, cycling and camping.

TOURIST INFORMATION
Luxembourg Tourist Office
Tel: 020 7434 2800
Fax: 020 7734 1205
Email: tourism@luxembourg.co.uk
www.luxembourg.co.uk

Pint-sized Luxembourg is largely overshadowed by its larger neighbours, sharing borders with Belgium to the west and north, France to the south, and Germany to the east. A tiny, landlocked territory, shielded from the sea by Belgium, Luxembourg's cross-frontier fraternization has nurtured a cosmopolitan, tri-lingual society that boasts the highest percentage of foreigners of any EU nation. The capital, Luxembourg-Ville, has a delightful, UNESCO-listed historic centre complete with turrets, towers and spires. The surrounding expanses of countryside are a scenic mix of rolling hills and lush valleys nestled amongst forests, rivers, vineyards and striking sandstone crags.

ARDENNES

Creepy-crawlies and communal showers can present certain challenges to a weekend of romance, yet a camping weekend needn't be 78 hours of cold feet and soggy mattresses. Sleeping under canvas can evoke a romantic, rustic feel where the allure is a connection with the natural world – as well as your camping partner. Couples don't need to rough it to camp proper, though. Pack a decent ground sheet, a proper blow-up mattress and pick a tent comfy enough to journey far from television, traffic, work and the stress of the daily grind. Free from the pressures of everyday life, you'll have the time and energy to focus on each other – even in the rain. Simply pack your wellingtons and waterproofs and indulge in candlelit board games and skinny-dipping under the stars.

More than one third of Luxembourg's territory is forested, a source of considerable pride for the Duchy's outdoor-loving population. Tufted peaks and fast-flowing rivers are looped by a spaghetti of leafy hiking trails in one of the most compact countries on the planet. Little wonder then that Luxembourg, sandwiched between Belgium, Germany and France, is home to hundreds of excellent campsites dotted through the countryside. A lengthy camping tradition ensures a growing array of options to suit couples, from two-man tents to luxurious yurts.

In the Ardennes region, at an altitude of 226 m (741 ft), campsites hug the boulder-strewn River Sûre under trailing branches. It is a camping idyll and wonderfully scenic – one of Luxembourg's most romantic 'under canvas' spots. On the grassy curves of the riverbank, campers wake to stunning views and a dawn chorus to peak out at an ethereal sunrise before returning to their cosy sleeping bags.

Transforming a functional tent into a couple-friendly boudoir is easy with a two-person self-inflating mattress and proper pillows and blankets offering maximum snuggle-factor. For guaranteed warmth and cosiness, pack a two-person sleeping bag in a suitable weight – choose one that is as thick as possible to keep out the weather during spring and autumn trips. Then open a bottle of wine and fire up the gas stove for a romantic supper – when you're camping, even scrambled eggs on homemade bread takes on a gourmet feel. And those worries about a muddy midnight dash to the loo? They will simply disappear in the candlelit glow.

CONTACTS
Camping Du Moulin
Tel: +352 99 03 31
Fax: +352 90 06 15
www.campingdumoulin.be

Enjoy a night or two under canvas before exploring the forested expanses of the Ardennes.

BELGIUM

TIME DIFFERENCE GMT +1

TELEPHONE CODE +32

CURRENCY Euro

LANGUAGES Flemish and French

POPULATION 10.3 million

SIZE OF COUNTRY 30,528 sq km
(11,906 sq miles)

CAPITAL Brussels

WHEN TO GO Low-lying Belgium is prone to
showers pretty much year-round. April to
September is drier, with July and August the
hottest and sunniest months when rooms are
more expensive and harder to come by. Winters
are generally wet and cold, but not bitterly so.

TOURIST INFORMATION
Visit Flanders-Brussels
Tel: 020 7307 7738
Email: info@visitflanders.co.uk
www.visitflanders.co.uk

Belgian Tourist Office
Tel: 020 7537 1132
Fax: 020 7531 0393
Email: info@belgiumtheplaceto.be
www.belgiumtheplaceto.be

Belgium's multicultural and multilingual flatland is punctuated with needle-thin canals, castles and cities. The northern agricultural regions are dominated by farmland pastures, by contrast with the largely urban central regions and the wooded plateaus to the south. Flanders, made up of the upper Dutch-speaking provinces, is proud of its fine art cities while French-speaking Wallonia, in the south, is characterized by the rolling hills of the Ardennes.

A fine brewing and confectionery tradition thrives in the cosmopolitan cities of Bruges and Brussels where over 300 homespun beers and some of most acclaimed and desirable chocolates in the world are produced. Belgium also boasts a sophisticated cultural and gastronomic life and is renowned for its jazz scene, cosy cafes and flower-filled festivals.

CONTACTS
Brussels Jazz Marathon
Email: info@brusselsjazzmarathon.be
www.brusselsjazzmarathon.be

*Visit Brussels in August when
the Grand Place is transformed
in a blaze of colour.*

BRUSSELS

Homespun Belgium musician Toots Thielemans beautifully captured the essence of romance through tender harmonica-led jazz melodies. His album, *Only Trust Your Heart*, combined his trademark playful style with passionate, deep undertones that run from soulful laments to heart-warming romps. With credits on a host of movie scores, including *French Kiss*, Thielemans' most notable solo appeared in *Breakfast at Tiffany's*, where his plaintive *Moon Rive*r in the opening scene brilliantly establishes the film's mood of romance noir. Yet Thielemans isn't a lone talent in Belgium's smouldering jazz tradition which, for a small country, has spawned some world-class maestros. In Brussels, the mellow strains of legendary jazz masters echo around thousands of cosy clubs and lounge bars nationwide. The craft continues to thrive, from Toots Thielmemans' sultry classics to a new wave of emerging talent at Brussels' mellow Jazz Rally and a host of big-band brunches and lunchtime Latino lilts.

At the city's Grand-Palace, the Bruxellois gather as they have done for centuries, celebrating festivals and enjoying the Sunday bird market in this oh-so-vibrant focal point – yet ensuring no task is more pressing than to sit, have a beer and let the world pass by to the sound of soothing jazz. In May each year, the Brussels Jazz Marathon takes centre stage here, attracting over 450 musicians to play 125 free concerts in the city's main squares, clubs and hotels. In August, the magic is elevated to spectacular levels when the cobble-stone streets of the Grand-Palace are transformed into a blaze of colour by a carpet of 800,000 fragrant begonias. This rich and sensual floral tapestry is heightened by the exotic breeze-swept perfumes. Grab a table at a pavement cafe to soak up the bloom-filled view before enjoying a Passion cocktail at the charming Hotel Amigo. To revel in the transatlantic musical romance between American and Belgium jazzmen check out the lobby lounge at Hotel Windsor where the tinkling ivories are attuned to a nostalgic impulse. A repertoire of ageless tunes include many of Toots Thielemans' most masterful ballads that serenade an appreciative clientele nightly (6–8pm).

041 BRUGES

CONTACTS
Guild of the Bruges Chocolatiers
Fax: +32 50 34 31 50
Email: info@brugsechocoladegilde.be

The Old Chocolate House
Tel: +32 50 34 01 02
www.oldchocolatehouse.com

Bruges Tourism
Tel: +32 50 44 46 46
Fax: +32 50 44 46 45
Email: toerisme@brugge.be
www.brugge.be

Try a shared bike ride to work off those chocolates through Bruges's streets.

Since the ancient Mayan civilizations, chocolate has been prized as a decadent indulgence. Heralded as a lure for lovers by the Aztecs, chocolate was initially consumed in gooey liquid form and hailed for its aphrodisiac qualities. When chocolate melts in the mouth it produces a rapid heart rate more intense than when engaged in passionate kissing. A favoured courtship gift, chocolate embodies romance and can heighten sensitivity and euphoria with its aroma. Today, as the producer of 172,000 tonnes of chocolate each year, Belgium is the undisputed King of Chocolate – a chocoholic's heaven. Home to over 2,000 chocolate shops selling a vast array of feather-light truffles and pralines, Belgium's

Theobroma Cacao (meaning 'God's cocoa food') is worthy of hushed prayers of thankfulness for the sensual pleasure of its consumption. Renowned for the high-grade sugar, creamy milk and rich cocoa that courses through its main arterials, Bruges is a city swathed in the rich aroma of chocolate year-round.

Weekenders can easily indulge in the unabashed pursuit of all things chocolatey, from tasting in at least a dozen forms to tours at the chocolate museum. Sniffing out Bruges's fine collection of chocolatiers is easy – simply follow your nose. A good place to start is Simon Stevinplein, a neatly paved plaza that is fast becoming the mustering point for chocolate fiends keen to discover the city's cocoa-laden heart. Freshly made Belgian chocolate at fair prices characterize this cluster of confectioners, with The Chocolat Line and Dumon both reputable names, each offering myriad varieties of truffles, pralines, chocolate squares and dark, milk and white chocolate treats. Choose from ribbon-wrapped, nut-encrusted chocolate gifts and cherry-topped chocolate sculptures, or select chocolate-rich biscuits, paper-wrapped marzipan chocolate and chocolate-dipped cookies and gingerbread.

Handmade Belgian chocolates are created with 100 per cent cocoa butter, and are fresh and preservative free. The Old Chocolate House is a respected practitioner that treats chocolate-making as an art. For hourly demonstrations and, most importantly, the chance to sample, head to Choco Story – the city's chocolate museum – before a cup of creamy hot chocolate at De Proeverie in Katelijnestraat. As befits a chocolate city, Bruges has its own official chocolate, the Bruges swan (*Brugsch Swaentje*) – made to a secret recipe. The city is also home to a four day Chocolate Festival, Choco-Laté, in spring each year – an event that every sweet-toothed connoisseur should enter in their diary.

NETHERLANDS

Low-lying Holland mixes its trademark national icons – windmills, clogs and tulips – with some less obvious Dutch treasures. Reclaimed polders and river deltas sit mainly below sea level while an extensive network of coastal dunes and levees run along the coast. Gentle slopes constitute Holland's upper ground in the foothills of the Ardennes in the east and south. The lush, green forest of Arnhem and the grassland landscape's crisscrossing rivers and canals offer a riddle of peaceful trails. Holland's cities offer a gamut of urban pursuits, from slow-moving river cruises and canal walks to picnics in the park.

TIME DIFFERENCE GMT + 1

TELEPHONE CODE +31

CURRENCY Euro

LANGUAGE Dutch

POPULATION 16.3 million

SIZE OF COUNTRY 41,864 sq km (16,327 sq miles)

CAPITAL Amsterdam

WHEN TO GO Springtime brings a rush of colour to Holland as tulips reach full bloom. Summers are generally dry, with sunshine peppered with rainy days, while autumn turns cool and winter is wetter, with cold and icy spells.

TOURIST INFORMATION
Netherlands Board of Tourism
Email: hollandinfo-uk@nbt.nl
www.holland.com

042 AMSTERDAM

CONTACTS

Toko Ikan Mas Indonesia
Tel: +31 6 18 45 98
Fax: +31 6 18 50 31
Email: info@ikanmas.nl
www.ikanmas.nl

Wielertaxi
Tel: +31 6 28 24 75 50
Email: info@wielertaxi.nl
www.wielertaxi.nl

Vondelpark
www.vondelpark.nl

Amsterdam's resplendent
Vondelpark is the perfect
spot for romantic seclusion.

It can be an unexpected sensual pleasure to experience the exotic heritage of Indonesia in a European city. Nestled between the ancient sea trading routes of Far East and Middle East, Indonesian culture owes its origins to a fusion of Hindu, Buddhist, Confucianist and Islamic influences. As a part of the Dutch East Indies until 1949, Indonesia's ties with the Netherlands remain steadfast in the nation's capital. Today, Amsterdam is a rich tapestry of a zillion Indonesian influences from shadow puppet theatres and Balinese massage to the pulsing rhythms of *dangdut* music and bold Javanese art. Yet it is the city's aromatic *rijstafel* (rice table) that epitomise Amsterdam's fusion culture, born out of a shared relationship between The Netherlands and Indonesia. Amsterdam's famous rice dishes (typically served with spiced fish and coconut milk curries) have been wholly claimed as a Dutch delicacy. Picnics in the park centre on a tapas-style array of *rijstafel* tasters while many popular fast foods forgo ketchup for rice and sambal, a hot, spicy sauce.

To experience the most delicious, freshly cooked *rijstafel* head to Toko Ikan Mas Indonesia, an Amsterdam institution that threw open its doors in 1984. Conveniently located in central Amsterdam, just a 5-minute stroll from the Van Gogh Museum, this pocket-sized eatery devotes itself entirely to take-out. A mile-long menu offers an array of flavoursome specialities, from spicy vegetarian stir-fried dishes to meat-loaded coconut noodles. Feeding everyone from office-workers and CEO's with lunch and early suppers, Toko Ikan Mas Indonesia is open 6 days a week (Monday to Saturday, 12–8pm). A multitude of different rijstafel menus offer the perfect meal to share at leisure. Simply order ahead, pack a blanket and hail a space-age *wielertaxi* (rickshaw) on the street for the 10-minute journey to Vondelpark, Amsterdam's resplendent urban green space. Seeking romantic seclusion? Then pick a leafy enclave by the bandstand: a favourite spot with picnicking couples amidst Indonesian deities, expansive woodlands and ponds.

CONTACTS
Logeerboot Rotterdam Kralingen
Watertorenweg 180
Tel: +31 6 55 18 64 73
Email: evet@bart.nl
www.logeerboot-rotterdam.nl

*Cosy up on a traditional
houseboat and enjoy
picture-perfect waterscapes.*

ROTTERDAM

When Noah designed his Ark his priority was practicality. When the Dutch created houseboats, comfort and cosiness were high on the list. Home to the densest network of waterways in Europe, Holland is renowned across the world for its 8,046 km (5,000 miles) of navigable canals, rivers and lakes. Travelling in the slow lane is a way of life here, be it in a sprawling metropolis or leafy rural terrain. Cruisers, barges and houseboats are moored amidst fine old cities, windmills, bulb fields, forests and extensive polder landscapes, offering unique views of Holland through portholes across urban backyards and canal bridges.

Vessels of the sea and inland barges are inextricably linked with Rotterdam; a port city perched on the banks of the River Nieuwe Maas, formed by the Rhine Delta. Named after the Rotte River, Rotterdam is one of Holland's most architecturally diverse and culturally eclectic cities born out of distinctive post-war reconstruction. Handsome harbour houses, sleek skyscrapers and spires rub shoulders with Rotterdam's funky cube houses, designed by Piet Blom. Hulking docks pay homage to a seafaring heritage while overhead the 185-metre (610-ft) high Euro Mast overlooks a collection of futuristic bridges, inner-city olden harbours, historic ships and glitzy

modern yachts. Climb aboard a wooden sailboat to journey past shipyards, take a wharf-side cruise or stroll along the portside to watch cargo-bearing, seagoing vessels and flotillas of sailing ships. Take a trip around the Maritime Museum to soak up Holland's rich naval heritage before enjoying fine waterscapes at Oude Haven, Rotterdam's trendy quay-side haunt. It was from here that the pilgrim fathers set sail for America in 1620.

Although Amsterdam is better known for its houseboats, Rotterdam has a fine – if small – collection of floating hotels from 95 Euros per night. Most are former working vessels once engaged in transporting sand, gravel and coal across Holland's many canals (*grachts*). One, owned by local character Eric van Emden, is moored in the Watertorenhaven area, near the vibrant Watertoren dockland district. Van Emden's painstakingly restored 1911 ferry is a labour of love that is high on luxury, comprising a beautiful, self-contained suite with bags of authentic nautical character. Forget all visions of damp, cramped, dingy quarters – this place is stylishly romantic and equipped with fluffy bedding and every conceivable high-tech mod-con. An MP3-dock allows guests to create their own mellow onboard ambience with gorgeous views from a spacious deck across the winding channel of the Nieuwe Maas.

DENMARK

TIME DIFFERENCE GMT +1

TELEPHONE CODE +45

CURRENCY Danish Krone (DKK)

LANGUAGE Danish

POPULATION 5.4 million

SIZE OF COUNTRY 43,094 sq km
(16,807 sq miles)

CAPITAL Copenhagen

WHEN TO GO Denmark has a temperate climate
with very little fluctuation between day and night
temperatures. February is the coldest month at
0°C (32°F) while warm, sunny summers can see
highs in the low 20s (68°F-plus).

TOURIST INFORMATION
Visit Denmark
Tel: 020 7259 5959
Email: london@visitdenmark.com
www.visitdenmark.com

The Jutland peninsula and the 400 lush green, windswept islands
that surround it form one of Europe's smallest countries: a nation that
links the rest of Scandinavia with continental Europe. Home to fine,
modern cities and fairytale castles, Denmark has its roots deep-
buried in the riches of the sea. Quaint fishing villages, boatyards and
maritime harbours spawn yachts, sail boats and fishing vessels
amidst waters that were once a Viking domain. Some 7,300 km
(4,526 miles) of coastline and 100 bird sanctuaries offer plenty of
natural beauty. No place in Denmark is more than 52 m (32 miles)
from the coast – a close land-to-ocean connection that permeates
every aspect of the Danish psyche – food, folklore and lifestyle.

CONTACTS
Odense Tourist Bureau, Funen
Tel: +45 6 612 7520
Fax: +45 6 612 7586
Email: otb@odenseturist.dk
www.odenseturist.dk

Visit Funen (Fyn)
Email: info@fyntour.dk
www.visitfyn.com

Egeskov Castle
Tel: +45 6 227 1016
www.egeskov.dk

Fairytale castles infuse Odense with whimsical romance.

ODENSE

The region of Funen (Fyn) epitomizes whimsical fairytale romance, offering hundreds of enchanting, medieval Rapunzel-esque towers on a backdrop of lush, flower-filled meadows. Dreamy moat-ringed castles topped with ornate spires characterize the landscape of Hans Christian Andersen's land of magical make-believe, and to journey through Funen is to travel through a storyteller's glorious picture-book. Denmark's circular 'Garden Island' sits in the centre of country, forming a convenient 2,985 sq km (1,164 sq mile) stepping-stone to bridge the channel between Jutland and Zealand. Captivating back roads weave past shimmering lakes scattered with birds and dragonflies amidst windmills, woodlands, pebbled beaches, bird-filled salt pans and half-timbered villages in bubblegum hues. As the time-worn inspiration for Andersen's literary delights, the region's gently contoured, hop-filled pastures and grand gated gardens remain steeped in the myths and legends of princes, princesses and fairies.

Funen's capital, Odense, offers more green space per head of population than any other city in the nation and boasts intimate, shrub-fringed cobbled plazas and gardens filled with vibrant blooms. Enjoy a romantic stroll along the winding Odense River where shoreside jazz musicians serenade a flotilla of slow-moving vessels. Afterwards delve into a dizzying array of cosy pavement cafés, bric-a-brac stalls and galleries before sampling delicious regional cheeses at bustling food markets Koncerthuset and Rosenbæk Gårdmarked. Odense's Hans Christian Andersen Museum celebrates the writer's beguiling tales, now translated into 150 languages around the world. And for a fitting finale, why not share a glass of Denmark's effervescent vintage, a tantalizing bubbly lovingly crafted by Sven Moesgaard, said to be a gift from Bacchus, the God of wine, and best enjoyed under a starry sky. At majestic Egeskov castle, a glass can be accompanied by the stirring heartfelt symphonic thrills of Funen-born composer Carl Nielsen. Marvel as a zillion dazzling fireworks explode over Europe's most splendid 450-year-old moat castle set amidst the most tender of settings – a maze of towering hedges, herbaceous gardens, yew trees, grandiose fountains and cupid-shaped topiary.

045

COPENHAGEN

CONTACTS
Summerbird Chocolaterie
Tel: +45 3 393 8040
www.summerbird.dk

Frederiksberg Chokolade
Tel: + 45 3 322 3635
www.frederiksbergchokolade.dk

Conditori La Glace
Tel: +45 3 314 4646
www.laglace.dk

Visit Copenhagen
Tel: +45 7 022 2442
Fax: +45 7 022 2452
Email: touristinfo@woco.dk
www.visitcopenhagen.com

*Pop-in-the-mouth sized
chocolates are the perfect
food for love in Copenhagen.*

To take a bite from Copenhagen's divine *Søde Minder* (sweet memories) tradition is to discover the very flavour of a city where over 200 confectioners purvey some of the finest patisserie in the world. Epitomised by a flaky delicacy so elegantly unobtrusive that it takes several nibbles to discover its hedonistic depths, the Danish pastry represents an edible metaphor for the city. A network of pedestrian streets harbours nearly a quarter of the nation's *konditorier* (coffee and pastry shops), confectioners, bakeries and tearooms where myriad confections promise to steal your heart. Behind Copenhagen's broad city squares, a tantalizing aroma of sweet-smelling backstreets wiggles across the city hemmed by rows of homely shops, their windows generously stocked with little cakes. Pastries topped with sugar icing sit high in porcelain display cases, cloaked in a thick aroma of chocolate, nuts and marmalade. Crumbly, honey-encrusted, chocolate-coated or glazed with fruit and delicately slathered in fondant, Copenhagen's sweet treats gleam like treasure.

Many of Denmark's finest confections have been made the same way since the 19th century when a strike by Danish bakers prompted an influx of replacement Austrian talent. Vienna's bakers brought with them recipes for millefeuille, or filoux pastry, which they learned to make from the French. Once the Danes had settled the dispute and were back at work, they acquired a passion and flair for the rich, light pastries, adopting the Continental dough and making it their own by adding yeast and sweet fillings. Today the city's confectioners turn out an eye-popping array of sugary baked goods, from giant pinwheels and braids to mouth-sized *kringles* (pretzel shapes) and delicious light-as-a-feather syrupy slabs.

Highlights include the charming *Conditori La Glace*, Denmark's oldest and most famous confectioner founded in October 1870. Today, this family-run, sixth generation concern in beautiful old premises creates award-winning cakes and pastries, such as tiny upside-down *urtepotte* (flower pots) of whipped cream, walnuts and blackberry rum, coated with chocolate, and the wonderfully rich, fondant-topped Othello cake.

Similar love and care is afforded to Copenhagen's Rubinstein cake, a decadent concoction of chocolate-covered cream puffs, whipped cream, cheese and rum adorned with nuts and cherries.

An important part of Copenhagen's sweet-toothed *Søde Minder* heritage is its fine chocolate makers with remarkable saffron-white, chocolate-filled pralines and chocolate-capped red berries; just some of the sumptuous treats. Famous chocolate guru Thomas Herman has even created a *Søde Minder* chocolate box containing his four favourite varieties, evoking Copenhagen's bygone age. Another master of chocolate innovation is maverick Rasmus Bo Bojesen, who trained in France under various Michelin-starred chefs, most notably the famous *chocolatier*, Bernachon. In a collaboration with Anton Berg, a Danish chocolate producer of long standing, Bojeson has produced a world-acclaimed, luxury chocolate filled with such unusual flavours such as thyme, Earl Grey, fennel, Ricard and chilli. Yet Copenhagen's most elaborate chocolate display is found next door to *La Glace*, where a traffic-stopping fountain is enough to make chocoholics gasp. You'll also find a scrumptious display of tiny treats filled with cream, truffle, fruits, liqueurs, spices and nuts – some of which can be sampled on request.

Speciality shops also produce Denmak's conical-shaped *kransekage* cake of almond paste traditionally served at celebrations, accompanied by coffee and a glass of brandy or Drambuie. Margarete cake, named in honour of Denmark's queen, is layered in chocolate cream, marzipan and berries while tiers of puff pastry filled with coffee cream characterises the delectable *Fasselitze*. Romantics seeking a fitting location in which to indulge their chocolate addiction should head to Frederiksberg Allé, Copenhagen's Parisian-style boulevard or to the quaint Old Town where up to 100 types of chocolate and pastries promise to satisfy every sweet tooth. Keen to pop the question or simply utter some words of love? Ask for a mouth-watering *Rødgrød* (red pudding) to share a heart-shaped white chocolate overlooking gardens, fountains and statues.

GERMANY

TIME DIFFERENCE GMT +1

TELEPHONE CODE +49

CURRENCY Euro

LANGUAGE German

POPULATION 82.5 million

SIZE OF COUNTRY 349,223 sq km
(136,197 sq miles)

CAPITAL Berlin

WHEN TO GO Germany's climate is almost as
varied as its culture, but extreme temperature
highs and lows are rare. Summers average
between 20 and 30°C (68–86°F), although
frequent showers can be unpredictable.
Winters are generally cold.

TOURIST INFORMATION
German National Tourist Office in London
Tel: 020 7317 0908
Fax: 020 7317 0917
Email: gntolon@d-z-t.com
www.germany-tourism.de

As Europe's sixth largest nation, Germany extends as far south as
the Alps, while the northern plains are riddled with northward-flowing
watercourses and bird-rich wetlands. On the French border, the
Black Forest divides the Rhine from the Danube's headwaters.
Glacier-formed lakes in the north-east date from the last ice age,
while central uplands soar and the coast offers more than 1,000 km
(620 miles) of beach. Wedged between Holland and Poland, to the
south of Denmark on the Baltic and North Seas, Germany is home to
pretty mountain villages, medieval fortresses, tumbling vines, majestic
castles, bubbling springs and a tangle of dark, mysterious forests.

BADEN BADEN

In a spa-town where bare flesh and wellness go hand-in-hand, Baden Baden's relaxed approach to clothing is suitably continental. Clothing isn't optional in the 130-year-old all-nude *Friedrichsbad* – it is surplus to requirements. So strip off, chill out and let the local health-giving springs work their magic on your stressed-out body. Baden Baden's ancient bathhouse has pampered the rich and famous in its elegant surroundings since the early 19th century, attracting couples from near and far. Today this steamy world of marble, brass columns, tropical tiles, herons, lily pads, and graceful nudity is practically unchanged. What's more, the waters of Baden Baden ('Bathing Bathing') are so good they named it twice.

Rejuvenating spa treatments and health rituals begin with a steamy, hot, invigorating shower. Next, step into warm air baths in vaulted, tiled chambers before another shower. Then, it is time for a brisk rubdown with a soapy brush until your skin glows so pink and clean it almost squeaks. After yet another shower, two stages of steaming thermal baths follow in succession before a final, cooler shower denotes the beginning of the next bathing stage. Men and women enter separately through opposite wings but, after a final cool shower, are reunited. Four restorative hot-spring baths follow requiring a shared nakedness with other couples, albeit in a sulphur-rich haze.

Each of Baden Baden's brackish pools varies dramatically in temperature, with the sequence in which bathing occurs an important part of the process. Men and women use the pools together: moving from one fog-cloaked cauldron to another in order to maximise the water's healing powers. Bathing help wash aches and pains away – as well as many of the awkward embarrassments of nudity. Couples appear more relaxed by the third stage. By the fourth, dinner plans are openly discussed by cascading waterfalls and the bird-filled trails of the Black Forest. Nudity, who cares?

Couples sharing in Baden Baden's health-giving waters will experience age-old spa rituals at their finest. Wrap up in a towel and plunge into the steam, then cuddle up in cocooned comfort in fire-warmed fluffy towels. Surrounded by charming Old World elegance, be lulled into slumber overlooking gardens of roses, rhododendrons and azaleas to the sound of gentle lullabies. Bodies softened, tensions soothed and minds relaxed.

CONTACTS
Friedrichsbad Spa
Tel: +49 7221 2759 20 / 40
Fax: +49 7221 2759 80
Email: info@carasana.de
www.carasana.de

Soothe your body and ease your mind in Baden Baden's über-relaxing spa baths.

BERLIN

CONTACTS
Avis Car Hire (Fun Car Division)
Tel: +49 3046 0601 0
www.avis.de

Schlosshotel Berlin
Tel: +49 3089 5840
Fax: +49 3089 5848 00
Email: info@schlosshotelberlin.com
www.schlosshotelberlin.com

Cruise through the streets of Berlin in your very own Porsche before heading for the open road together.

Famously modelled on the female form, the Porsche 911's seductive curves nip in at a waspish waist before rounding out to womanly contours. Synonymous with high-powered romance and glamour, to drive behind the wheel of a Porsche is to enter a dynamic world of power, prestige, playfulness and elegant poise. A Porsche's masculine side is embodied in a throaty engine rumble while a slick, light-as-a-feather thrust evokes the aura of feminine grace. German-designed for pure driving enjoyment, a Porsche can be driven on every type of road surface rain or shine. No need to drive flat-out pedal-to-the-metal in order to experience its ultimate pleasures, simply touch, feel and absorb the unity of being wholly in-tune with the machine.

Revved up by such stars as James Dean and Steve McQueen, Porsche's image is one of sensual glamour. Coax it into acceleration to pound the super-sleek German autobahns or idle along leafy country lanes to explore Berlin's romantic royal castles and storybook Gothic towers in style. According to Porsche purists, the more miles you cover in a 911, the deeper the affection grows – so settle back behind the steering wheel, and let the love flow.

Unlike other high-performance sports cars, a Porsche is built to drive well under the mixed speed traffic conditions of a normal road, not just a speedway track, though Germany's speedy *Autobahns* certainly allow plenty of opportunity to rip up the asphalt. However a Porsche can potter around town and journey comfortably just as expertly as it can reach nought-to-sixty in 5.5 seconds. It can also be left outside in the rain and snow overnight without worry; come the morning, your Porsche will still purr like a cat.

Founded in the late 1940s by talented car designer Ferdinand Porsche, the basic Marque has evolved through air-cooled 'flat six' engine

911 models to the latest water-cooled 996 (911) designs. Porsche remains a proud symbol of stylish German automotive ingenuity to be found in innumerable showrooms country-wide. Romantic weekenders can also hire a Porsche 911 from a number of local car rental agencies, including Berlin's upscale division of Avis. Simply stump up 199 euros per day and drive off the forecourt in the latest open-top model to journey to the city's little-known turrets, citadels, ruins, follies and palaces with the wind in your hair.

Outer-Berlin's landscape is straight from the Brothers Grimm: mysterious forests, medieval castles in the air and fabled rivers. Fairytale towers tell stories of ancient loves in enchanting gardens dotted with sparkling lakes and spouting fountains. One of the most beautiful castles in Berlin is the Charlottenburg Castle, the largest palace in the region and named after Queen Sophie Charlotte. Commissioned by King Frendrick II, the original 17th-century Italian Baroque structure was expanded several times during the early 18th century to add an orangery and a new wing on

the castle's eastern side. Walks around the castle are plentiful and provide breathtaking views across the gardens to the mausoleum and the earlier tea house, known as the Belvedere, which has some amazing collections of pottery and porcelain.

Other romantic highlights include Glienicke Palace set amidst an ensemble of parks, gardens and palaces created by the landscape architect Peter Joseph Lenné. Elements of Classical and Byzantine art and architecture are integrated into the palace and its gardens, underlining its Mediterranean character. Meander through spell-binding gardens to stunning river- and lakeside walks to the Havel River. Gilt lions modelled after the Villa Medici fountain in Rome decorate a large fountain in front of the main façade with the romantic leaf-shrouded *Klosterhof* (cloister yard) deserving of shared contemplation.

In the centre of Berlin, the 18th century *Prinzessinnenpalais* (the Palace of the Princesses designed by Friedrich Wilhelm Dietrichs) has served as the residence for a number of different members of the Prussian ruling family. Almost destroyed during World War II, the palace has been restored to its former glory with a richly decorated interior and lavish opera hall. A short, enjoyable journey out to the Pankow district of the city allows an opportunity to witness this, one of Berlin's most marvellous examples of Baroque architecture, set in resplendent gardens near the Panke River. In 1740, Friedrich II gave this property to his wife, Elizabeth Christine, and much of the original furniture and decoration from this era remains. After World War II, the castle was used as the formal seat of the President of GDR. Today, it is owned by the Prussian Palaces and Gardens Foundation Berlin-Brandenburg.

Make your last port of call, the sumptuously built *Schlosshotel* (Castle Hotel), a lavish former grand mansion and seat of the von Pannwitz family in 1914. Renowned throughout Germany for its extravagant banquets for 1,000 guests, waited on by 200 servants, today the *Schlosshotel* retains a rich, palatial charm evocative of bygone splendour. Karl Lagerfeld, guru of haute couture, has embued the romantic interiors with his unmistakable style, whilst valet parking ensures there is plenty of space in which to cosset a Porsche.

048

CONTACTS
Munich Tourism
Tel: +49 89 2300 180
Fax. +49 89 2300 1811 1
Email: tourismus@muenchen.de
www.muenchen.de

*Munich's Christmas Market is
an enchanting scene, redolent
with olden-day charm.*

MUNICH

Munich's pre-Christmas preparations transform the city into a spellbinding magical wonderland where carols and harp music fill the air and child-like excitement reigns supreme. Signalling the beginning of Advent, an array of baubles and twinkling fairy-lights engulf every building amidst life-size Christmas nativity scenes, fir trees and giant holly wreaths. To meander through Munich's thrilling festive spectacular is to absorb some of its captivating Yuletide romance. Painted wooden curios, handmade toys and sprigs of berries dangle from ledges and windows. Frosted fairies and snow-covered elves rub shoulders with Bavarian brass bands to the tantalising sound of tinkling sleigh-bells. Stalls laden with marionettes, candles and lambskin shoes nestle amongst a mouth-watering aroma of cinnamon-baked apples, marzipan and chestnuts.

Germany's Christmas enjoys a centuries-old tradition that reaches back to the Middle Ages when regular seasonal markets took place throughout the year. During the bitter cold-weather months, the pageantry and spirit of the Christmas markets were a welcome distraction from the long, dark winter. Snow-weary villagers found joy in gathering together with their neighbours in Yuletide celebration. The year 1642 saw the arrival of Munich's first Christmas Market and today the city's festivities retain a strong traditional character. Local handicrafts, delicious regional foods and candy owe nothing to mass-production and come with plenty of old-fashioned Christmas cheer.

At sundown, the markets take on a fairytale magical splendour as Alpine lanterns and candles flicker under a moon-filled, snowflake sky. In a confetti-like flurry, traders, artisans and wood-carvers warm their hands around wood-burning stoves while gingerbread (*Lebkuchen*) vendors ply for trade around towering Christmas trees covered in tin whistles and candied fruit. Sizzling sausages, thick potato pancakes (*Reiberdatschi*) and jugs of hot spiced *Gluhwein* help to keep the cold at bay while rosy-cheeked children place sugar-sprinkled letters on their windowsills for *Christkind* – a winged figure charged with distributing Yuletide gifts. Bag-laden shoppers wrapped in thick woollen coats and scarves yield to the hustle and bustle of the Marienplatz: a mesmerizing scene that evokes an enchantingly festive and romantic atmosphere amidst the spinning carousels.

AMORBACH

Formerly part of the estate belonging to the Benedictine Abbey of Amorbach, the Schafhof of Amorhof looks back on a long historic tradition dating back to 1445. The Abbey's brethren overcame the outside forces of romance, politics, power and professional ambition to remain unified by love and belief. They toiled, prayed and ate together joined by a close-knit bond as a unique collective, rich or poor, noble or peasant. Growing fresh produce in neat gardens, they stored fruit, vegetables and grain and upheld a rule never to turn away a passing stranger. The building was lovingly rebuilt in 1721 and further restored in 1974 after falling into disrepair when the brothers moved on. Today, the Schafhof continues the tradition of Benedictines in welcoming newcomers to a place of tranquil relaxation in the now homely former monks' chambers. Combining romantic charm with the comforts of the modern age, a well-stocked kitchen garden continues to yield fresh crops to fill a pantry, cellar and storehouses with preserves, brandies, honeys and wines.

Located in the heart of the Odenwald amidst the rolling plains of the Rhine rift surrounded by wooded thickets and dark green, tufted slopes, the old Monastery sits in a region blessed by nature. Sparkling rivers and freshwater streams offer a magnificent backdrop for exploration amidst some of the purest air in Germany, whatever the season. Winter allows for a romantic sleigh-ride through the snow-covered foothills along Odenwald's 10,000 km scenic trails. In summer, blueberries, strawberries and mushrooms fill the forests, whilst a sign-posted *Apfelwein* trail snakes through fruit meadows and orchards. Dozens of local cider producers and wine-makers offer ample opportunity to sample their wares from large stone-glazed jugs with a blue motif (*bembel*). Consume it neat like the purists or mix it with fizzy water to produce a light, refreshing *Panzersprit* to use as a romantic toast in place of sparkling wine.

On the matter of love, Benedictine Monks mused that: 'Romance feeds on possibility and withers when the outcome is a foregone conclusion', and in Odenwald that element of surprise is in rich supply – especially where *Apfelwein* is concerned. Symbolising Union, Faithfulness and Good Luck in the local romantic folklore, this potent apple liquor is also steeped in fertility legend – it is considered to be a powerful aphrodisiac.

CONTACTS
Schafhof Amorbach
Tel: +49 9 3739 7330
Fax: +49 9 3734 120
Email: rezeption@schafhof.de
www.schafhof.de

Soaring woodland characterizes the unspoilt Odenwald.

050

HAMBURG

CONTACTS

ATG Alster-Touristik GmbH
Tel: +49 4 0357 424
Fax: +49 4 0353 265
Email: info@alstertouristik.de
www.alstertouristik.de

Hamburg offers a captivating story of sentimental nostalgia and elegant romance.

If the heart of Hamburg is its bustling harbour, then the Alster River is its soul, formed by a tributary of the River Ebe in the 13th century to become the core of the city's everyday life. Split in two during the 17th century to create the park-cloaked, 160-hectare *Außenalster* (Outer Alster) and promenade-lined 18-hectare *Binnenalster* (Inner Alster), the Alster waterway offers a unique perspective from the water on Hamburg's pleasing panoramas, in peaceful contrast to the hubbub of the city. Cruise past towers, church spires and the beautiful woodlands of Alster Park and its handsome riverbank buildings and gleaming sailboats. Follow the storied course of the river to learn about its ancient myths and legends under the gaze of the city's impressive bridges and historic docks. Since it was dammed in the Middle Ages, the Alster River has taken on the shape and curves of an expansive lake, hugged by many of Hamburg's grandest structures together with aged, rope-strewn quays.

In addition to the standard short cruise to Rundfahrt, a longer river trip meanders past the historic villas and gardens of the city's elite to Hamburg's imposing 19th-century warehouse district that lines the canals of the old working port. Waterborne Hamburg offers a captivating story of sentimental nostalgia and elegant romance interspersed with plenty of modern, 21st-century glamour. In the midst of this green Hanseatic city, the River Alster is a paradise for the city's boaters, oarsmen and paddlers and embodies the 'togetherness' of the city as its most popular meeting point. Sip a glass of Hamburg's famous *Alsterwasser* – a mix of German beer and lemonade, and as refreshing as the river itself on a summer's day – as you glide along the Alster's languid stretches. For extra romance, choose a twilight cruise to absorb sunset panoramas and magical views with a glass of Champagne. Hamburg's lamp-lined waterways take on a breathtaking intimacy as night falls and the star-studded skies illuminate the city. Cruises run March to October and depart from Jungfernstieg with two-person charters available for romantics seeking the ultimate on-the-water soiree at dusk.

CONTACTS
First Limo
Tel: +49 7 1150 0044 7
Fax +49 7 1150 0044 8
Email: info@firstlimo.de
www.firstlimo.info

Castle Hotel Hornberg
Tel: +49 6 2619 2460
Fax: +49 6 2619 2464 4
Email: info@berg-hotel-hornber.de
www.castle-hotel-hornberg.com

*Few experiences can match
a private helicopter tour over
this stunning city.*

STUTTGART

Though renowned for its urban intensity, Stuttgart's magnificent green spaces bring startling contrasts to the city's futuristic, metropolitan hub. Stuttgart's concealed charms may not unfold immediately yet those prepared to seek them out will discover a dazzling panorama. Encircled by a ring of smaller settlements, the city of Stuttgart sprawls across innumerable hills, valleys and parks set within a beautiful, lush valley enclosed by forest-covered slopes and orchards. As the capital of Baden-Württemberg, Stuttgart is also blessed with some fine traditional architecture, with pretty houses set on stepped terraces (*Stäffele*) nestling between vineyards and the River Neckar. A puzzle of geo-thermal underground canals surges with mineral-rich, spring-fed waters close to the jutting peaks of the magnificent Swabian Mountains and the Black Forest's mysterious fringes. The region, dubbed the Stuttgart Cauldron for its steam-shrouded, bubbling intensity in the heat of summer, sits amidst vast castle turrets and noble gardens – a romantic interlude from Stuttgart's urban heart.

Stuttgart's lesser-known to-die-for views are best relished from above and the city's fine array of luxury air transport options offers plenty of choice. Few craft can traverse the city's airspace with the deft precision of a helicopter high atop Stuttgart's traffic-congested streets. A number of tour companies run personalised tours across the city's main architectural highlights. Others provide tailored options to suit individual itineraries and budgets, adding in floral bouquets, wine and chocolates for a romantic touch. Encircle super-swish banking districts, shopping malls and Stuttgart's famous Mercedes plant before skirting forested walking trails that loop the curves of the city's leafy surrounding slopes.

Follow the winding course of the River Neckar and marvel at the statuesque 19th-century palaces on a metropolitan terrain dotted with hidden Cold War former military hubs, Baroque mansions, Romanesque spires, Gothic arches and post-war towers. For the ultimate romantic treat, follow the Neckar northward to the wooded Neckar Valley (*Neckartal*) where idyllic hills evoke a lost time past. Standing above a wide curve of the river the 11th-century Castle Burg Hornberg stands sentinel over passing barges and, since 1953, has operated as a restaurant and hotel. Original towers sit atop a steep-sloped mountain, surrounded by vineyards and vast stone gates on the riverside. Choose a table on the open air terrace overlooking the spectacular valley for a gourmet menu and local fine wines in the setting of medieval knights and truly romantic views.

052 FRANKFURT

CONTACTS
Touristik-Arbeitsgemeinschaft
Romantische Straße
Tel: +49 9 8515 5138 7
Fax: +49 9 8515 5138 8
Email: info@romantischestrasse.de
www.romantischestrasse.de

*Discover doll-like half-timbered
villages amid a fairytale
landscape of valleys and spires.*

In the 1950s, travel agents coined the name *Romantische Straße* (Romantic Road) to better describe southern Germany's 360 km (224 mile) stretch of nostalgic highway, and the name is apt. Dozens of prettily coloured, half-timbered villages beg further exploration allowing an *über*-romantic cross-region road trip against a backdrop of plunging valleys and soaring spires. Hire a Mercedes, pack a picnic and stick on a suitable soundtrack to cruise along Germany's finest thematic routes through Bavaria's medieval heartland. Pass Renaissance castles, Rococo churches and fantasy palace towers in a quintessential German panorama. Running from Würzburg on Bavaria's northern tip with its beautiful, UNESCO-status Baroque romance to Fussen on the Austrian border, the Romantic Road follows the course of the winding River Lech.

Served by both Munich and Frankfurt airports, the route skirts the magnificent 120 km (74 mile) Tauber Valley (*Tauberfranken*) embedded in forests and meadows and framed by vineyards and softly waved slopes. Blessed with innumerable historical testimonies to over a thousand years of history, art and culture, the Tauber Valley region is home to some of Germany's most beautiful architectural treasures. Visit the castle ruin of Wertheim, the monastery of Bronnbach, the Baroque wine-trader houses of Tauberbischofsheim, Bad Mergentheim's grand palace of the Teutonic Order and the opulent domain and flower-filled gardens of the Hohenlohe dynasty. Yet it is the medieval walled city of Rothenburg ob der Tauber overlooking the Tauber Valley that best symbolises the Romantic Road's seductive spirit, with its series of beautifully preserved towers and riddle of narrow, cobbled streets. Climb stone-stepped stairwells to ascend the ramparts at the Roedertor tower at the east end of the city for gasp-inducing views across Rothenburg ob der Tauber, a town seemingly untouched by time.

Car hire agents at Frankfurt airport offer a good line in top-end Mercedes from around 125 euros per day. While it is possible to drive the full Romantic Road in around five or six hours, most road-tippers prefer to linger a little longer to discover the Spanish Baroque palaces of Schillingsfürst, Feuchtwangen's famous 12th-century Romanesque cloisters and Dinkelsbühl's romance-filled alleyways. A tunnel takes you straight under Schloss Harburg, one of the most carefully preserved castles in Bavaria – a thrilling fairytale spectacular. A sign for Mad King Ludwig's fantasy castle in Schwangau near the Bavarian former monastery town of Fussen heralds the last of the *Romantische Straße's* jewel-like clusters – and the end of the road.

AUSTRIA

Breathtaking mountain scenery and magnificent rivers characterize Austria's natural riches, from the Alps in the west to the Danube Basin in the east. Snow-topped peaks and gingerbread-style Alpine chalets typify the country's picture-postcard ski regions while Austria's bustling cities – from ornate capital Vienna, and Salzburg, Mozart's birthplace, to Innsbruck's dramatic backdrop as the gateway to the Austrian Alps – mix historical splendour with world-class museums, opera houses and galleries.

Landlocked Austria shares its borders with eight countries – Switzerland, Liechtenstein, Germany, the Czech Republic, Slovakia, Hungary, Slovenia and Italy. An enduring reputation for music, literature and the arts is peppered with influences from neighbouring cultures, both ancient and contemporary, yet Austria's classic Alpine landscapes remain seemingly untouched by time.

TIME DIFFERENCE GMT +2

TELEPHONE CODE +43

CURRENCY Euro

LANGUAGE German

POPULATION 8.19 million

SIZE OF COUNTRY 83,858 sq km (32,705 sq miles)

CAPITAL Vienna

WHEN TO GO Two distinct seasons affect rural tourism. Mountain resorts, for example, have a winter sports calendar and a season for summer hikers. In between times, many tourist facilities are closed. Urban centres are popular year-round, with tourist numbers swelling during peak holidays and annual festivals. Visit during May–August for the best of the warm weather, while snow is pretty much guaranteed November until early April.

TOURIST INFORMATION
Austrian Tourist Office
Tel: 0845 101 1818
Fax: 0845 101 1819
Email: holiday@austria.info
www.austria.info

CONTACTS
Innsbruck Tourism Office
www.innsbruck-tourism.at

Fiaker Carriage Rides
Tel: +43 1 96 602 61
Email: info@fiaker.co.at
www.fiaker.co.at

Take a laid back approach to sightseeing in Innsbruck with a horse-drawn carriage tour.

INNSBRUCK

Innsbruck's carriage rides take on a magical feel in winter when plummeting temperatures coat the city in a sugar-like frosting. Delicate sunshine sends rays dancing across a silvery cityscape laced with an icy nip where passengers are treated to horse-drawn journeys wrapped in thick, warm lap blankets and woven shawls. Innsbruck's traditional four-wheeled horse-drawn *landau* owes much to 18th-century German ingenuity and French design. Built for social jaunts, these big-bellied carriages offer a smooth, rolling transit at a graceful pace. Elliptical suspension guarantees a reassuring level of comfort with facing seats set over a dropped foot-well across a swept base on a single flowing curve. At the front, a driver sits on an upholstered bench-seat, surveying the route and mapping the road ahead. In polished ceremonial-style harnesses, his four steeds trot along in elegant synchronicity, breath exhaling like kettle-steam in Innsbruck's crisp, cold air.

Hailing a horse-drawn carriage (known as *fiaker* after the Parisian Rue de Fiacre where they were first popular) in Innsbruck is as easy as strolling to the doors of the city's iconic Landestheatre – you'll spot them in a neat line along the kerb. Choose from a set-time city tour or ask for a special two-hour romantic route (from around 290 euros including sparkling wine; canapés and soft drinks are an extra 60 euros) for an enchanting tour full of old-fashioned charm with the Nordkette mountain ridge visible from every second street corner. Clip-clopping hooves and the slow-whirring clacks turning wheels add to this most nostalgic of Innsbruck sight-seeing experiences, past larger-than-life bronzes, Baroque churches, stucco-encrusted Rococo buildings, grand arches, memorials, boulevards and pretty, paved squares. Warmed by a mug of *gluhwein* (hot red wine and mulled spices), there is something wonderfully woozy about a horse-powered meander through Innsbruck at sunset when temperatures freefall spectacularly to sub-zero levels. For a touch of extra romance, explore the city's outlying villages to spot Austria's snow-topped 'honeymoon huts'. Set aside for sweethearts, these old hay barns are steeped in age-old fertility legends – the locals swear a couple may enter as two but will always leave as three.

VIENNA

Once deemed too risqué to be danced by unmarried couples, the sinfully close embraces of the Viennese Waltz earned it persecution for vulgarity. Originally a folk dance, the waltz was born out of peasant yodelling tunes and eventually given a name derived from the German *walzen*, meaning to roll, turn or glide. It finally gained some moral respectability following the French Revolution, when attitudes on Europe's uptight dance-floors loosened. Today, couples all over the world enjoy Vienna's spirited 180 beats-per-minute romps using time-worn dance steps to embark on a romantic voyage. The use of home-grown maestro Johann Strauss's *The Blue Danube* in the 1968 film *2001: A Space Odyssey*, further popularized the waltz. Over forty years on, Vienna's jovial whirling jaunt continues to captivate couples keen to master its charm and mystique.

Unlike the sluggish pace of its more sedate English cousin, the Viennese Waltz is a fast-tempo rotary dance packed with change steps and turns that require light, nimble footwork. Frequent clockwise (natural) or anti-clockwise (reverse) steps demand plenty of agility while stamina is essential to maintain floorwork at a rapid rate. With excellent tips and tuition, however, almost any Cinderella and her prince can go to the ball, according to the city's waltzing kings. And nobody in Vienna wants to be caught, come November's celebrated ball season, unable to move with finesse.

Austria's capital hosts hundreds of balls during a dazzling three-month season, when more than 300 events issue gilded invitations city-wide, and Vienna's *Musikvereinssaal* concert hall transforms itself into a swish chandelier-bedecked ballroom for the oh-so prestigious Philharmonic Ball. Hosted by an organization, guild or institution, each ritzy event attracts luminaries from the arts and film worlds – all with a shared adoration for Vienna's super-charged waltz. Lehar's melancholic *Gold und Silber* hails the final frolic of the night.

Before the ball season begins, all manner of newbie dancers and refresher students seek the guidance of Thomas Schäfer-Elmayer, a judge on Austrian TV's *Dancing Stars*. Each 50-minute instruction session encourages twirling with ease whilst providing an abundance of practical know-how, such as how to avoid toe-treading.

Expect to pay 200–500 euros for a ticket, be sure to dress to impress (white tie and tails for men and floor-length ballgowns for women), and alight from a fairytale horse-drawn carriage for the ultimate romantic splurge.

CONTACTS
Vienna Tourist Board
Tel. +43 1 24 555
Fax +43 1 24 555 666
Email: info@wien.info
www.wien.info

Elmayer Dance School Ball
Tel: +43 1 512 7197
www.elmayer.at

A waltz is the ultimate in old-school romance.

055

CONTACTS

Tourismusverband Fuschl am See
Tel: +43 6 22 682 50
Fax: +43 6 22 686 50
www.fuschlseeregion.com

An inspirational, romance-inspiring Swiss scene.

GRAZ

Whether we admit it or not, most of us can sing at least a few lines from Rodgers and Hammerstein's enchanting 1965 musical epic *The Sound of Music*. Even the sourest critic became enraptured by the film's breathtaking Alpine scenery, while a feel-good musical score captured hearts across the world with its exultant lyrics, ecstasies and tender refrains. From the stirring opening bars of 'The Sound Of Music' and Captain Von Trapp's tear-jerking 'Edelweiss' to the poignant closing bars of 'Climb Ev'ry Mountain', it is near-impossible not to be swept up in the romance of this charming tale of love. Against the breathtaking backdrop of Salzkammergut's glorious snow-capped peaks under vast, sapphire-blue skies, Maria and the Captain share a deepening bond. "For here you are, standing there, loving me, whether or not you should... Nothing comes from nothing; nothing ever could," they sing, amidst undulating Alpine meadows scattered with pine trees and gloriously coloured wildflowers.

Today, Salzkammergut's Fuschl am See remains an unspoilt mountain wonderland characterized by sparkling, gin-clear lakes and lush, green forests. The ancient Iron Age salt mines that gave Salzkammergut its name (*Salz* means 'salt') hide amongst soaring white-topped peaks and rippling fir-clad slopes. Delightfully secluded bays, conifer thickets and white-shingle beaches nestle amid 900 km (558 miles) of bird-filled hiking trails that sprawl in an orderly jumble via snowy summits, foothills and grass-hemmed shores. During the winter months the region's plunging valleys are transformed into some of Austria's most beautiful, when fresh white powder cloaks the countryside and log cabins warmed by fires emit a homely glow. Springtime brings birdsong and a riot of vibrant colour as shrubs begin to bloom and fresh shoots sprout in green mountain pastures. Melting snows bring magnificent cascading waterfalls that tumble over rocks and crags in some of Europe's purest, most invigorating air. During the summer months, the aroma of newly cut hay intermingles with harvest rituals and the traditional Austrian folksong of the countryside, while butterflies shroud the shimmering waters of Fuschl am See Lake. Autumn brings a mellow romance as the countryside readies itself for winter under a blanket of crimson-red, orange and gold.

CONTACTS
City Hotel Wolf-Dietrich
Tel +43 6 62 871 275
Fax +43 6 62 871 275 / 9
Email: office@salzburg-hotel.at
www.salzburg-hotel.at

Two-night breaks start from
209 euros per person

*An illuminated waterside awaits
– if you can bear to leave your
Love Bird suite.*

SALZBURG

As one of a growing list of countries across the globe to embrace the concept of a romantic in-room hotel picnic, Austria has seized on its potential. Menus are a fascinating cross between an upscale delicatessen, florist and couples' spa offering an array of scented massage oils, aromatic candles, bubble baths, gourmet food platters, vintage Champagne and romance-themed audio-visual delights. Providing couples with the ultimate romantic rendezvous, these so-called Love Bird suites ensure an idyllic mix of 5-star hotel luxury and uninterrupted togetherness. No need to dress for dinner, brave the cold and crowds or queue for a table or taxi; picnicking in a Love Bird suite boasts all the decadent touches of a fine romantic night out.

In Austria's romance-filled historical narratives the art of penning love letters is a recurring theme, in which suitors fulfilled their heart's romantic desires through powerful love-fuelled prose. Perfumed, hand-scripted messages conveyed desire and longing while endearingly crafted epistles offer declarations of life-lasting love.

At Salzburg's Hotel Wolf Dietrich, the romantic potency of the pen is celebrated in beautifully created boudoirs that take the concept of Love Bird suites to another level. The décor at this cosy family-run hotel takes on an opulent Louis XIV feel complete with sweeping drapes in the balconied rooms. Giant beds piled with plump pillows sit under a sky of starry lights atop a fragrant carpet of velvety pink rose petals. Gleaming bathrooms stocked with perfumed oils and sumptuous robes open up onto an expansive lounge beautifully illuminated by candles and aromatic lanterns.

"You bring nothing but love, peace, joy and happiness to my soul," read the heartfelt words that claim their place around a library of romantic literature, CDs and DVDs. Slushy? Yes, undoubtedly: yet the Hotel Wolf Dietrich manages it with impeccable grace and good taste. Together with the cupids, hearts and flowers, the suite contains a small stock of reading material of a decidedly more sensual and erotic nature. A careful feng shui design claims to maximize sexual chemistry, while an organic menu unfettered by chemicals or additives is dedicated to a food experience that will make a body feel good. Choose from a suite with a spiral staircase offering rooftop views across Salzburg or a garden setting complete with trailing vines, blooms and nymphs.

CZECH REPUBLIC

TIME DIFFERENCE GMT +1

TELEPHONE CODE +420

CURRENCY Czech crown

LANGUAGE Czech

POPULATION 10.2 million

SIZE OF COUNTRY 78,866 sq km
(30,758 sq miles)

CAPITAL Prague

WHEN TO GO The Czech Republic is situated
in a temperate zone and boasts four distinct
seasons of equal length. Winters are relatively
mild (at around -2°C/28°F) and summers rarely
exceed 22°C (72°F).

TOURIST INFORMATION
Czech Republic Tourist Office
Tel: 020 7631 0427
Fax: 020 7631 0419
Email: info-uk@czechtourism.com
www.czechtourism.com

Split into two distinct geographical and cultural portions, the Czech
Republic is characterized by the spa towns of Bohemia and the
wine-growing villages of Moravia along with over a hundred castles,
fortresses and fine chateaux. Almost a thousand kilometres of way-
marked trails crisscross mountains, valleys and lakes that are sun-
blessed during summer and snow-covered in winter. Low hills roll
into basin plains and rivers stretch out across borders towards the
sea. The country is also home to some of the most beautiful cities
in Europe, from the dazzling Art Nouveau, Baroque and Neo-
classical splendour of Prague on Central Bohemia's River Vltava to
medieval Brno.

CONTACTS
Romantic Prague
Tel: +420 233 375 333 /
+44 (0)7956 416 164
Email : info@romanticprague.com
www.romanticprague.com

A romantic stroll across the Charles Bridge spells classic romance.

PRAGUE

As the throbbing heart of central Europe, Prague has long enjoyed a history of romance offering a lover's dream with its winding cobblestone roads, antique horse-drawn carriages, charming intimate restaurants and cosy hotels. As the golden city of spires, Prague fuses a breathtaking mix of Romanesque, Gothic, Medieval and Baroque architecture spanning a thousand years. Nothing says 'fairytale' like a castle on a hill, and Prague has just that. Towering over the River Vltava, Pratske Hrad dominates the grand Hradcany royal complex, where Renaissance and Rococo facades juxtapose over pretty plazas. Romantics keen to embrace an age-old tradition descend on Old Town Square on the hour to tuneful chimes of Prague's 600-year-old astronomical clock. Meander in the footsteps of nobility through the Royal Route across the Old Town Square, passing the Baroque palaces of the Lesser aged streets that boast a richly storied past. Stoll past the resplendent Gothic church of Our Lady of Tyn to a labyrinth of narrow backstreets steeped in an enchanting legend amidst picturesque architecture seemingly untouched by time. To walk across quaint Charles Bridge is to be transported to a bygone era – little wonder the city was voted the 10th Most Romantic City on the planet by honeymooners, according toTheKnot.com

Couples keen to absorb Prague's romantic atmosphere will find plenty of hidden hideaways in which to cosy up. Several dedicated tour companies in the city offer packages that cater to true romantics, from all-inclusive weekend breaks for love-birds to elaborate marriage proposals complete with every conceivable cupid touch. All manner of romance-inspired services are available for anniversaries, engagement ceremonies and vow renewals – with at least a dozen ways of popping the question. Anything is possible, from Champagne-filled baths and vintage limousines to intimate dinners, spa pampering, hand-picked gifts to treasure, sunset river cruises, handmade jewellery and rose-scattered pillows. They'll even organise a luxurious surprise picnic on the banks of the mighty Vltava River or in one of Prague's gorgeous tree-lined parks – with a classical string-quartet to serenade your partner. Simply choose your favourite wine and special song and pick the perfect spot for the ultimate romantic gesture – RomanticPrague.com will do the rest, be it a floral bouquet or front-row opera tickets.

058

BRNO

CONTACTS
Brno Tourist Information Centre
Tel.: + 420 542 210 762
Fax: + 420 542 423 963
Email:info@ticbrno.cz
www.brno.cz

Brno Philharmonic Orchestra
Tel: +420 542 218 284
Fax: +420 542 218 284
www.filharmonie-brno.cz

Music has a powerful effect on virtually every aspect of human behaviour, be it love-making, birth, marriage or death. In classical music, particularly, enharmonic key changes and tonal shifts can influence our moods while musical pulses have a proven effect on heart rates. Slow rhythms provide relaxation, slowing heart rate and promoting rest as in soothing lullabies, while up-tempo beats heighten our levels of excitement via peptides in the brain that stimulate endorphins. These natural opiates have a mesmerizing, euphoric effect that can energize muscles as well as alter mood and emotions. In the Czech Republic, this strong physiological influence on the body is evident in Brno – the nation's philharmonic capital, where an illustrious history of music-making has exploited the power of melody on human emotions for centuries – to dramatic effect.

Since the 1870s, the Brno Philharmonic Orchestra has wowed audiences with adventurous rhapsodies and free-flowing suites from a magnificent purpose-built auditorium in the city, Besední dum. Pushing musical boundaries, the orchestra has continued to strive to tantalise every sensory switch. Using delicate flute solos, melodic horns and a volley of notes on the marimba, the Brno Philharmonic Orchestra prides itself on evoking emotion and physiological effect.

Romance permeates many of the orchestra's musical themes, from the robust pungent chords of heartbreak to heightened ardour in the form of creeping chords and rising scales. Urgent, sometimes dizzying and continually surprising orchestral performances run from calm harmonies (a gentle kiss) to tempos that border on breathless (frenzied passion) to silvery strings of wondrous delicacy (a tender embrace). Three International Music Festivals offer a compelling array of passion-filled classics by great Czech maestros, such as Dvorak, Korngold and Smetana. The largest, Brno International Music Festival, wows a sell-out crowd during dozens of dazzling events, recitals and full orchestral concerts in venues throughout the city. As the Czech Republic's leading musical collective, the Brno Philharmonic Orchestra stages around 65 concerts each year in

Brno together with dozens of acclaimed performances ithroughout the Czech Republic and the world. In 2008, the Philharmonic were bestowed the honour of opening the prestigious Prague Spring Festival, while in 2000 they staged a concert at the Vatican for Pope John Paul II. Since an inaugural world tour in 1956, the Orchestra has toured across six Asian countries, played over 700 European venues and performed regularly in the US, collaborating with such distinguished conductors as Karel Ancerl, Jiri Belohlavek, Sir Charles Mackerras, Kurt Masur and Yehudi Menuhin.

Janácek's second string quarter, *Intimate Letters*, evoked his relationship with Kamila Stosslova and is a romantic drama that carries a sharp emotional charge. Janácek was twice Stosslova's age yet became utterly infatuated with her, writing of her: "in your company one's spirits are lifted; you breathe warm-heartedness, you look on the world with such kindness that one wants to do only good and pleasant things for you in return. You will not believe how glad I am that I have met you." Inspired by the 700 letters they shared, *Intimate Letters* is an ecstatic outpouring of emotion from a man wracked with passion for a younger woman. Fulsome melodic flurries whirl us from their first fateful meeting, through blissful dedication to a mournful lament on what might be and a final glorious explosion of trills – a seriously challenging work for any quartet. The completion of the piece prompted a further note to Stosslova in which Janácek declared: "I am just overwhelmed by the sheer warmth of this work of ours, this quartet". Today this deeply moving composition enthrals audiences world-wide, depicting the joys of love with a shivering, spine-tingling musical eloquence. *Intimate Letters* officially premiered in September 1928, in Brno, a month after Janácek's death.

In Brno, music is synonymous with romance.

SLOVAKIA

TIME DIFFERENCE GMT +1

TELEPHONE CODE +421

CURRENCY Slovak Koruna

LANGUAGE Slovak

POPULATION 5,423,567

SIZE OF COUNTRY 48,845 sq km
(19,050 sq miles)

CAPITAL Bratislava

WHEN TO GO Bloom-filled April and May brings
zest and vigour to Slovakia after what are typically
cold, dark, cloudy winters. Bright, cool and breezy
summers are ideal for outdoor pursuits, with
sunshine that runs well into September and
October.

TOURIST INFORMATION
Slovakian National Tourist Office
Tel: +421 48 413 61 46
Fax: +421 48 413 61 49
Email: sacr@sacr.sk
www.slovakia.travel

Slovakia's resplendent mountains rise in the hills of the Malá Fatra
and run east to the Alpine peaks of the starkly beautiful High Tatras.
Renowned for its coniferous forests and sulphur-rich curative
springs, Slovakia shares its borders with Austria, the Czech
Republic, Hungary, Poland and Ukraine. Magnificent plunging
valleys, glassy lakes and a puzzle of downhill ski runs lead to pretty,
flower-filled orchards and traditional villages. Umpteen aged fairytale
castles hide amongst grassy rolling hills and woodlands edged by
swathes of tumbling vines.

PIESTANY

According to legend, it was the iridescent blue-green or green-coloured plumage of an elegant but lame peacock that first revealed the magical powers of Piestany's spring-fed water sources. Discovered by the waterside, the injured bird had dragged itself towards the springs but was limp and near exhaustion. Stunned by its beauty, the villagers gently lowered the bird into the waters to bathe its dull, lacklustre sheen. The peacock was miraculously cured; fanning its wings to display its tail feathers in all their shimmering glory to the wonderment of the crowd. Today, as a sacred bird of the Greek goddess Hera, the peacock symbolises Piestany's curative claims of eternal youth and embodies healing and restoration.

Located in Western Slovakia in Trnava County, on the banks of the River Váh, Piestany's age-old therapeutic waters and clay-rich soils are renowned through Eastern Europe for their all-ills cures. First settled in 1113, Piestany flourished during the early Middle Ages when a monastery first started organised bathing in its sulphuric-rich, milky-white pools. Rising to temperatures of 67–69°C, the waters boast a chemical composition conditioned by the geological stratification of the Povazsky Inovec Mountains, rich in gypsum–sulphuric properties. Similarly, Piestany's bath-warm mud is formed from tiny claylike particles and swept into thermal wells. Hot, steamy and shrouded in a creamy haze, the water is rich in organic sediment and health-giving natural bacteria. A reputation for wellness grew, and soon the bubbling hot mud, clay sediment and brackish spring-waters were being harnessed to aid convalescence and good health. At the end of the 18th century, spa buildings were constructed complete with fountains and spouting springs, earning Piestany international repute. Financiers, artists, athletes, politicians and doctors were drawn here on account of the waters' restorative qualities and during the mid-20th century Piestany was used by Austro-Hungarian servicemen during the First and Second World Wars. Visitors arrived jaded, cynical and dead-on-their-feet and left bright-eyed, radiant and revived. Today many fine, historic spa buildings continue to administer hydro-therapeutic R&R from a menu of over 60 traditional treatments, from mineral mud baths, hot-mud body wraps, water-pressure massages and herbal foot baths to hot stones and nutrient-rich clay facials.

With Piestany's eternal youth-giving peacock as its crest, the Hotel Thermia Palace enjoys resplendent views across the park-scattered Spa Island, the town's pretty, garden-ringed, curative epicentre. Built in 1912, this fine Art Nouveau building sits directly atop a rich subterranean thermal source. Umpteen rejuvenating therapies reflect the romantic facade of this palatial structure offering old-time elegance and a touch of modern spirit with a focus on preservation and longevity. Over 100 rooms include 15 romance-inspired suites packed with ceramic detail, wood panels, stained glass and peacock-inspired frescoes. A balneotherapy centre designed over a hundred years ago by legendary spa architects Ármin Hegedüs has required only partial renovation. Today it evokes the nostalgia of a romantic bygone era experience in centuries past by poets, sheiks, maharajahs, writers, kings and princesses.

CONTACTS
Thermia Palace Health Spa
Tel.: +421 33 775 6111
Fax: +421 33 775 7739
Email: reservations@spapiestany.sk
www.spapiestany.sk

Find wellness and rejuvenation in the company of a loved one at Piestany's spas.

POLAND

TIME DIFFERENCE GMT +1

TELEPHONE CODE +48

CURRENCY Zloty

LANGUAGE Polish

POPULATION 35.8 million

SIZE OF COUNTRY 312,684 sq km
(121,947 sq miles)

CAPITAL Warsaw

WHEN TO GO Poland's weather is unpredictable,
with winters that vary dramatically in intensity from
mild to bitterly cold. However, summers are
generally warm and the most pleasant time to visit,
with July the hottest month. September turns cool
as October approaches, with colder weather
increasing until December when the temperature
drops below zero – sometimes to -20°C (-4°F).

TOURIST INFORMATION
Polish National Tourist Office
Tel: 08700 675 012
Fax: 08700 675 011
www.poland.travel

Poland's 500 km (310 miles) of coastline trims the Baltic Sea to the
north in an unbroken rolling stretch while the Carpathian Mountains
dominate the south. Bordered by seven countries – Germany,
Russia, Lithuania, Belarus and the Ukraine to the north and the
Czech Republic and Slovakia to the south – Poland's varied mix of
climates is greatly influenced by its neighbours. Chilly polar breezes
bring icy blasts from Russia and Scandinavia while warmer gusts
travel in from the south. Wildflower pastures and fast-flowing rivers
lead to pretty mountain trails and hilltop villages just a stone's throw
from major cities.

GETTING THERE
2½–3-hour transfer from
Warsaw airport

CONTACTS
European Boating Holidays
Tel: +44 (0)845 450 5229
Email: info@eurobh.com
www.europeanboatingholidays.co.uk

*Evoke the carefree romance
of times past in Poland's
lake district.*

MAZURIA

Northern Poland's vast lake-scattered region is dubbed 'the land of a thousand lakes', yet with upwards of four thousand lagoons, the description hardly does it justice. The Masuriaan Lakes have few equals in Europe, stretching across several thousand square kilometres to contain over a quarter of all the freshwater in Poland, including the famous Lakes Âniardwy and Mamry. Bordered by Russia, Lithuania and Belarus, Poland's north-easterly corner boasts extraordinary scenic beauty: an enchanting land of postglacial splendour, dotted with otherworldly geological features and comprising a network of lakes, canals and rivers fringed by great swathes of pine, oak and silver birch forest. A nature-lover's paradise, the region boasts a rich fauna of lynx, deer, bison, wolves, wild boar and beavers as well as a wide range of birds.

Until the Second World War Mazuria was part of East Prussia, steeped in the ancient folklore of 13th-century Teutonic Knights. Today crumbling hill-top castles offer telltale mementoes of a past era in the ancient settlements of Gizycko, Worgorzeno and Ryn. Extensive woodlands provide a network of mysterious wildlife-rich walking trails littered with remnants of a Gothic era. Numerous peninsulas, islets and coves clad in a near-impassable tangle of forests are protected by several natural reserves with a combined area exceeding 1 million hectares. Steep-sided hills lead to plunging valleys, rocky troughs and ridged, glacial synclines; scrubby, exposed plains strewn with peat bogs and shallow marshes are rich with butterflies and medieval relics. And a 126-km-long canal linking Elblsg and Ostróda boasts a century-old system of locks that embodies waterborne romantic adventure.

Cruising boats have explored this region since the 1920s when the region became synonymous with carefree summers of bathing, fishing and waterside picnics. Today, numerous boat tours run from the historic town of Mikolajki, an attractive waterfront settlement founded in the 18th century. Meander southwards to Ruciane and cross Lake Sniardwy's vast expanse to the ancient castle town of Pisz. Travel north to pass under the swing bridge of Gizycko (opened for boating traffic five times a day) and cruise towards the captivating, Baroque-style settlement of Sztynort. Set on a peninsula between Lake Mamry, Lake Labap and Lake Kirsajty, Sztynort's grand, 18th-century fairytale palace hides amid wooded parklands and evokes the romantic charm of gallant knights – a must-visit destination for all romantics.

KRYNICA-ZDRÓJ

CONTACTS
Krynica-Zdrój Tourism
Tel: +48 18 471 55 22
Email: centralna-rezerwacja@
krynica.com.pl

*Enjoy rejuvenating spa
therapies against a soaring
Alpine backdrop.*

Dubbed the Pearl of Polish Health Resorts, Krynica-Zdrój embodies genteel 19th-century charm in its refined boarding houses, fountain gardens and handsome pump rooms. Rising up from deep, subterranean sources rich in mineral deposits, the waters of Krynica-Zdrój and its mild, sub-Alpine microclimate are synonymous throughout Poland with therapeutic soothing. Splash amongst the waters in the plant-decked spa buildings or lie in deep, 200-year-old pools of serenity in a historic string of old spas that prescribe good health via ancient curative recipes. Stroll amongst the healing chambers of the underground salt caverns or relax amongst the lush, green gardens famous for their health-giving fragrances and fresh, pure air.

As one of Europe's most scenic mountain regions, Krynica-Zdrój enjoys magnificent pine-topped panoramas looped by a network of Alpine streams and trails. Since its ancient, mineral-rich waters were first discovered, Krynica-Zdrój has been at the forefront of espousing the health benefits of the earth's powerful natural resources. Dozens of spring-fed wells offering various degrees of mineral composition form the basis of restorative and preventative wellness philosophies of which mind, body and soul are the focus. Babbling streams and sparkling springs tumble from the crisp, cool highland regions to bubble up in the valley's fine, historical wood-and-brick spa buildings.

Using natural therapies of hydro-massage, dry carbonic bathing and nutrient-rich mud, Krynica-Zdrój draws on all-organic CO_2 gases produced in its underground well system. Choose from nourishing mud compressions and clay-rich rejuvenating wraps or simply immerse yourself in the silken, chalky, oxidized waters of Krynica-Zdrój's regal, pillar-ringed bathing pools. Follow the soothing steam-cloaked cleansing rituals of yesteryear to detoxify the pores and the spirit. Sulphur and magnesium deposits help tired, aching limbs become a thing of the past as tension eases. Knotted muscles unfurl after a slow wade through giant whirlpool baths where the waters caress the skin in blissful motion. The skin softens and joints become supple as the body is sulphated, carbonated, fluorinated and pummelled. Revel in invigorating high-pressure jets that harness the region's therapeutic energies and experience the re-mineralizing effects of curative warm-water dips in lightly-fizzing, calcium-rich tubs. Delight in Krynica-Zdrój's delicate ozone bubbles and sensual all-over steaming, nestled in an oasis of romantic fluffy blooms against a majestic backdrop of mist-capped mountain peaks.

CONTACTS
Zamek Jan III Sobieski Hotel
Tel / Fax +48 58 673 88 05
Email: rzucewo@zameksobieski.pl
www.zameksobieski.pl

*Enjoy the shared experience
of horseriding on the shoreline
at Puck Bay.*

GDANSK

While Poland's near-century-long communist rule made all aristocratic pursuits impossible, the simplest equestrian pleasures remained all-important. The horse was essential and studs thrived across Poland's lush, green savannahs. Extensive European trade brought to Poland horses of all extractions: Hungarian, German, Dutch, Danish, Friesian, English, Spanish, Moravian and Italian, with horses widely interbred. 'The life of a Pole was lived in the saddle, and for him indeed "a horse was half his well-being"', wrote Erika Schiele in her 1970 book, *The Arab Horse in Europe*. 'He was so much one with his horse that it was like part of him – hence the Polish saying: "a man without a horse is like a body without a soul".'

Almost all of the common horse stocks were bred 'under the sky' on rolling plains of fertile soil similar to those of Hungary. Fed on rich steppe grass that made for rapid breeding, Polish horses fulfilled the role of transport, currency and companion. Before directed breeding, no definite Polish species had been established. However, the great hussar cavalry horse, primarily of eastern blood, changed Poland's fortunes, generating sizeable profits and kudos. Beautiful and graceful yet surefooted and unafraid, the genuine Polish equine gene pool was soon highly sought-after across the world. Today, EU statistics show that horse breeding, riding and racing represent an important segment of the GDP of Poland while many Poles readily admit to loving their horses more than their relatives. Far from the elitist sport of the rich, Poland boasts an open affection for its horses and sightseeing in the saddle. Tourists can follow thousands of bridal paths to explore fields, mountains and forests, either on an athletic thoroughbred Arabian or small, strong, cross-country Huculy. Discover the unspoilt shoreline of Puck Bay on horseback along a spine-tingling route that is hopelessly romantic, stretching from a handsome, cliffside, neo-Gothic castle owned, pre-Second World War, by the noble Von Below family, down to the Baltic Sea. Absorb a striking panorama across the bay and the Hel Peninsula, rimmed by leafy parklands planted by Polish King Jan III Sobieski, and dozens of romantic picnic trails.

063

POZNAN

CONTACTS
Lubuskie Log Cabin
Tel: +48 95 755 70 55 /
+48 60 499 10 28
Fax: +48 61 648 21 35
Email: office@angielski.co.uk
www.angielski.co.uk

Prices from 200 euros per week

A cosy log cabin is the perfect place to savour some time alone together.

The people who populate Western Poland's bucolic wonderland, the Lubuskie Lake District, have been characterised throughout time by their selfless kindness. Warm, generous and good-natured, the locals have a time-worn saying: *Potrzeba wiele serca, aby tylko troche kochac* – meaning you have to have a big heart to love a little. Just what has shaped the Lubuskie disposition, nobody rightly knows, but as a border region with Germany, an hour from Berlin's hubbub, the region boasts a hybrid of Prussian, Czech, Polish and German influences. Today it retains the timeless innocence of a bygone era with hundreds of centuries-old lakes that sparkle much as they did in years gone by. Thousands of hectares of ancient beech and pine forest are filled with rare birds, flowers, wildlife, fruits and berries, spanning 13,984 sq. km – five times that of Luxemburg.

In keeping with the Lubuskie love of the simple life, the delights of this scenic lakeland region are best enjoyed from a log-built cabin nestled in the woods. Typically set close to a river, this traditional, fuss-free Polish style of accommodation owes much to rustic country living, with the largest concentration found around Miedzyrzecz, Glebokie, Lubra, Lagow and Wilkowo. On the doorstep, a mix of bird-rich spruce and deciduous forest houses beavers, foxes, eagles, cormorants, swans, grey herons, corncrakes, cranes, ruffs, double snipe, storks and wood grouse. Lakes are full of carp and giant catfish and offer excellent kayaking through narrow channels under trailing branches.

Cosy log-burning stoves warm cooler nights with hammock-slung terraces for sun-drenched afternoons amidst a resplendent and secluded natural setting enveloped in peace. Crack open a bottle of home-brewed *cydr* (cider), the ancient brew of rural frontier towns in Western Poland, as you look out onto glassy, reed-hemmed waters surrounded by the lush, green, berry-filled habitat of wild boar, deer and bison. Most cabins have an outdoor grill and an iron-ringed fire-pit – the perfect spot in which to cook up the white sausages of the region. Gather wild strawberries in the dwindling light to the screeches of bats and rustles of roosting birds. Then serve up delicious hunks of sausage with Polish bread, mustard and bowls of *bigos* (spiced cabbage). It's a comforting and unpretentious banquet – much like Lubuskie is itself – accompanied by a soothing cicada chorus.

LITHUANIA

A land of lakes, castles and forests, Lithuania, located on the eastern Baltic coast, shares borders with Belarus, Latvia, Poland and Russia. Lithuania's 100 km (62 miles) of coastline boasts tree-fringed beaches popular with summer picnickers while the scenic shores of the Curonian Lagoon are riddled by bird-filled trails. Lithuania's hot, dry summers offer great potential for swimming in sparkling freshwater streams and lakes. Vilnius, in the southeast of the country, remains the least known and visited of the three Baltic State capitals, despite its beautiful and superbly-preserved historic core and outlying ancient castles.

TIME DIFFERENCE GMT +2

TELEPHONE CODE +370

CURRENCY Litas

LANGUAGE Lithuanian

POPULATION 3,575,439

SIZE OF COUNTRY 65,300 sq km (25,467 sq miles)

CAPITAL Vilnius

WHEN TO GO Summer and spring (May through to September) are warm and sunny, although the midsummer holiday (in June) sees crowds swell. July and August draw international visitors while many locals are on holiday. Winter (November to March) brings snowfall and only a few hours of daylight each day.

TOURIST INFORMATION
Lithuanian National Tourism Office
Tel: 020 7034 1222
Fax: 020 7935 4661
Email: info@lithuaniatourism.co.uk
www.lithuaniatourism.co.uk

GETTING THERE
Trakai is located about 15 miles
west of Vilnius

CONTACTS
Trakai Tourist Information
Vytauto street 69
LT-21001 Trakai
Tel/fax: + 370 528 519 34
www.trakai.lt

Trakai Castle is open daily.

Visit Trakai Castle for a medieval
spectacle reminiscent of
chivalrous times past.

VILNIUS

Even closet romantics can't help but be swept away by the pomp and pageantry of medieval jousting. A tournament pursuit dating back to the 11th century to keep armour-clad knights in prime condition during times of peace, jousting is a chivalrous challenge for a lady's honour that evokes the romance of Sir Galahad and Sir Lancelot mounted on thundering steeds. Plumes waving, chainmail clanking and ten-foot lances fully charged while maidens swoon with handkerchiefs pressed to their cheeks. Jousting kings and princes compete alongside rank-and-file jousters, unseating opponents in the fight for glory and the admiration of the fairer sex. Ladies would grant 'favours' to their chosen knights in the form of ribbons and other tokens. These were worn on the sleeve in battle before this most romantic one-one-one combat commenced; a gallant spectacle in which hearts would melt, or break.

In Lithuania, the joust and its romantic splendour are celebrated annually at Trakai Peninsula Castle in June, attracting brethren knights from all over the world. Trakai, the 14th-century capital of the Grand Duchy of Lithuania, boasts a rich martial tradition steeped in armour, weapons and Lithuanian monarchs. A romantic symbol of charismatic sovereignty and power, Traki Castle signifies the well-preserved spiritual heritage of Lithuania's Middle Ages and provides a rousing backdrop of fortifications, bridges, towers and battlements. Even the awe of the castle, a magnificent water-wrapped structure of towering blood-red brick, is heightened by shields and tunics, armour, medieval tents, 14th-century bows, arrows and quivers, breastplates, maces, stables and squires. Visitors can stroll around the reed-trimmed Lake Galve, or take a small pontoon boat over the moat, before crossing the vast wooden drawbridge set amidst Lithuania's only preserved historical park. The grand turrets of Trakai Castle transport visitors back through 600 years to when the Grand Duke Gediminas first laid a stone in this unassailable Gothic fortress. The romance continues in the castle's plush interior, with stained glass, murals, wooden galleries, secret stone passages and fabulous treasures. Although largely destroyed, the castle was painstakingly restored in the 19th century to become one of Lithuania's most-visited historical and architectural monuments. Star of romantic films, costume dramas and fairytale television weepies, Trakai Castle rises up amongst the region's 200 lakes, of which the deepest (46.7 m/153 ft) is Galvë with its necklace of 21 magical ancient isles.

LATVIA

Latvia's extraordinary biodiversity is determined by its geographical position in the western part of the eastern European plain. Set on the east coast of the Baltic Sea, Latvia's mixed forests and haze-shrouded, brackish waters enrich the serene Gulf of Riga with numerous surrounding fertile bogs and fens. A wildlife-rich terrain is home to nesting birds, flowering plants and ferns in a beautiful countryside setting studded with sparkling lakes. The 900-year-old capital city, Riga – once revered across Europe as the 'Paris of the North' – balances a handsome maze of cobbles and spire-adorned architecture with easy access to a jumble of scenic, flower-filled villages and leafy coastal trails.

TIME DIFFERENCE GMT +2

TELEPHONE CODE +371

CURRENCY Lats

LANGUAGE Latvian

POPULATION 2.5 million

SIZE OF COUNTRY 64,589 sq km (25,190 sq miles)

CAPITAL Riga

WHEN TO GO Latvia's prime tourist season runs from April to September, with July and August the most crowded months. From October to March, Riga's streets are reclaimed by the locals. Midsummer is highly popular with domestic tourists, so accommodation needs to be booked in advance.

TOURIST INFORMATION www.latviatourism.lv

065

RIGA

CONTACTS
Rita Tourism Centre
Tel: +371 67 026 072
Fax +371 67 026 068
Email: rtkic@riga.lv
www.rigatourism.lv

Discover the pull of the fern flower deep in the woods near Riga.

According to Baltic mythology, the enchanting fern flower boasts mysterious powers. A symbol of love and fertility, the exquisite fern flower (*paparades zieds*) is steeped in centuries-old Latvian folkloric tradition. Said to bloom on a single night, the fern flower is inextricably linked with the outdoor celebrations of the summer solstice. At this time, Latvians head to the countryside to revel in green hills, woodlands and crystal-clear rivers gushing through valleys. During the national holiday of Ligo (23 June) and Jani (24 June) sleep is spared as families gather for joyous festivities. It is also a time for lovers to declare their intent and cement their union. Traditionally, wreaths are worn using brightly-coloured blooms for females and oak leaves for males, in respect of the compelling forces of nature. It is now that the boundaries between the physical and spiritual worlds are at their most delicate, according to fortune-tellers and mystics. Houses are adorned with rowan branches, fresh herbs and birch twigs in elaborate Midsummer displays. Women make cheese; men brew beer while children sing and dance. Yet the solstice is synonymous with couples flushed with *amour* – and the fern flower's magic.

Paradoxically ferns aren't, in fact, flowering plants, although the Latvian myth is thought to have its roots in reality. Reports of a fern-like shrub with flowers that open after dark have been substantiated by botanists. Even in contemporary Riga, where traditions have slowly been eroded, the ritual of straying into the forests (*mezs*) at night-time is a well-observed courting ritual. Latvian forests provide a mix of northern coniferous and southern deciduous trees, with pine thickets, linden trees and a diverse spectrum of other species. On the outskirts of the city, Jani-fires are set ablaze on higher ground, using torches made with tar-soaked, straw-covered poles. Lovers entwine in the firelight to purify their souls. They also jump over bonfires, lit from sunset till sunrise, to ensure lasting love. Holding hands, the courting pairs then set out to scour the forest depths at Mezaparks for the elusive fern flower (a byword for a kiss and a cuddle). During the Jani celebrations, conception rates soar, resulting in a birthrate spike nine months later – all thanks to the magical powers of the fern flower.

ESTONIA

Located on the eastern shores of the Baltic Sea, Estonia is the most northerly of the three former Soviet Baltic republics. Low, flat and partially forested, Estonia has a shallow 1,393 km (864 mile) coastline dotted with 1,520 outlying islands. The country's highest point, Suur Munamägi (Egg Mountain) reaches 318 m (1,043 ft) above sea level in Estonia's hill-covered southeast. Rolling, tufted meadows are home to over 8,500 lakes, pools and rivers that feed large wetland expanses. Tallinn, Estonia's largest centre and capital city, packs a powerful cultural punch: its charming UNESCO-listed old quarter is already gearing up for its role as the 2011 'Capital of Culture'.

TIME DIFFERENCE GMT +2

TELEPHONE CODE +372

CURRENCY Estonian Kroon

LANGUAGE Estonian

POPULATION 1.3 million

SIZE OF COUNTRY 45,226 sq km (17,638 sq miles)

CAPITAL Tallinn

WHEN TO GO Estonia's temperate climate is characterized by warm summers and fairly severe winters, with year-round breezes from the Baltic Sea. Summer temperatures average 21°C (70°F) with July the hottest month. Winters can be severe with temperatures of -8°C (18°F) on average, although drops to -23°C (-9°F) aren't uncommon.

TOURIST INFORMATION
Estonia Tourism c/o Estonian Embassy
Tel: 020 7589 3428
www.visitestonia.com

CONTACTS
Voru Spa & Tourism Bureau
Tel: +372 785 09 01
Fax: +372 785 09 02
Email: vlv@vorulinn.ee
www.vorulinn.ee

*Enjoy Tallinn's stunning
cityscape in the early evening.*

VORU

Depending on who you ask, Estonian saunas are crucial to your love life, an important health ritual, a way to keep clean, or an unbeatable hangover cure. Yet, for most visitors, the Estonian sauna represents an unbeatable way to relax and rejuvenate. After a winter foray into the bone-chilling extremes of the snow-covered Estonian terrain, it is also a great way to thaw out. The Estonian rural sauna tradition extends from the Baltic region to the Urals – and dates back over 700 years. Today, it remains an intrinsic part of modern life: be it in courtship, friendship, wellbeing or matrimony.

Estonia's country folk saunas are character-packed rustic wooden huts that offer a traditional form of 'connection' with nature. Leave inhibitions at home, pack a bottle of local brew and pick your sauna companion wisely as you will be holed up together naked in a hot-and-sweaty tight squeeze for at least an hour. Typically, Estonians heat their saunas to 80–100°C – sometimes higher – so if you're unused to saunas pick a low, relatively cooler bench on which to perch for a gentle start. Heat rises so upper benches are hot enough to frizzle tender limbs like a well-seared rump steak –

lay a towel and approach with caution. Gently ladling water from a wooden bucket (*leil*) over scalding stones peps up the heat slowly but surely – a little-and-often, gradual process that shouldn't be rushed. Beating your partner's back with birch branches (*viht*) constitutes circulation-boosting pampering in Estonia – not a kinky act. So feel free to engage in this toxin-ridding ritual to experience a warm glow across the body, but wait until you're sweating profusely – the heavier the perspiration flow, the better.

Estonia's most common old-style saunas are heated by wood-fired stoves with hot stones on top. The water vaporizes in an instant, due to the extreme heat, causing the wooden structure to emit a pine-fresh fragrance in the steam. Smoke saunas were once viewed as terribly old-fashioned, but are now experiencing a resurgence in popularity – especially in cozy, country lodges. Housed in log-built cabins, a smoke sauna is distinctive for its high benches and chimney pipe. The room is filled with smoke and heated for a full two days using burning alder and while most of the smoke is emptied before use, it's still an eye-stinging experience akin to sitting in a carbon-spewing, sooty BBQ pit. For a more sophisticated ritual, Tallinn offers city-slickers plenty of upscale sauna options, from funky party sauna booths and temple-inspired steam sanctuaries to contemporary sauna-houses. In this sauna-obsessed city, the Old Town is home to a Sauna street and a medieval 'Sauna Tower'. Estonians think nothing of spending whole afternoons or weekends in saunas with family and friends and theorize the practice evolved as a sun substitute. Certainly, the intense heat provides some of the psychological benefits of sunshine during the long, dark months of the year. Many Estonian's consider a sauna the appropriate venue for a first date.

Estonia's Sauna Country is Voru in the southeast of the country, a 2 1/2 hour drive from central Tallinn. Here, early Estonians installed saunas in hillside caves and caverns. Today a number of old agricultural settlements open up their elderly saunas to weekenders in search of some rural R&R. Expect to pay around 1,500 kroons (£60) for an afternoon in a traditional farm sauna, including some Estonian beer (a caveat on the sauna ritual is drinking beer – before, during, and after. Beer is even sloshed on the rocks to fill the sauna with the smell of freshly baked bread).

An initial sauna session shouldn't exceed ten minutes at which point it is time to cool off – Estonian style, of course. In winter, this means running naked outside to roll in a snow drift or jump into an ice-cold lake nearby. However, in the absence of snow or natural water, a sub-zero shower is a decent alternative and serves to close those sweat-drenched open pores. Then rub a sticky-but-moisturising raw honey blend into the skin (and that of your partner) using juniper twigs as least as hot as the sauna itself. Touch the legs first, then the arms and chest – and important sequence for courting couples. According to Baltic legend, a host of love spells are cast in the sauna, so the heart should always be touched last – and tenderly so.

Experience a rejevenating shared sauna.

RUSSIA

TIME DIFFERENCE GMT +2/GMT +3

TELEPHONE CODE +7

CURRENCY Ruble

LANGUAGE Russian

POPULATION 142 million

SIZE OF COUNTRY 17,075,200 sq km
(6,659,328 sq miles)

CAPITAL Moscow

WHEN TO GO Russia's humid continental
European climate turns subarctic in Siberia and to
tundra in the polar north. Summers vary from hot,
dry and sunny to cool and breezy along the Arctic
coast, with sticky city micro-climates and
windblown rural expanses.

TOURIST INFORMATION
Russian National Tourist Office
Tel: 020 7495 7570
Fax: 020 7495 8555
Email: info@visitrussia.org.uk
www.visitrussia.org.uk

As the world's largest country, Russian has a very diverse geography
with most of the country's landmass nearer to the North Pole than
the equator. At around twice the size of the United States, Russia
encompasses around an eighth of all the inhabited land on the
planet. The route north to south spans an inhospitable route covering
4,500 km (2,790 miles), from the northern tip of the Arctic isles to
the Republic of Dagestan's southern nub. Some fourteen countries
share Russia's 57,790 km (35,830 mile) border – the world's longest
– from Asia through Europe to North Korea, China and Mongolia.
Home to thousands of lakes, a dozen seas and part of three oceans,
Russia's vast tundra, forests and grasslands, border mountains and
towns and cities, including the capital Moscow, is almost a country
in itself.

CONTACTS
Vladimir Kozyrev
Tel: +7 791 66 85 26 93

Renting a *dacha* costs 1,000 euros
per week or 150 euros per night.

*Cosy up together in your
own Hansel-and-Gretal-style
country cabin.*

MOSCOW

For centuries, Russians have counted down the days of winter until the arrival of the green shoots of spring. As the snow begins to fade away, the new season brings with it fresh verve and excitement as Moscow's city-dwellers prepare to journey the traffic-clogged beltway to reach the countryside's rustic pleasures. For according to local tradition, spring is the time when urbanites dust down their *dacha* (garden house) in readiness for the warm romantic glow of summer. Though *dacha* season runs from May until October, planting starts in early March when seedlings are placed in containers on windowsills in Moscow as soon as the wet, bare soil first allows. Ritual, hobby and an age-old lifestyle for tens of millions of Russians, the *dacha* symbolizes the simple riches of the so-called land-owning poor. Structurally it may be just a cabin, or sometimes even a shack, but spiritually a *dacha* is much, much more than that. On a garden patch, small orchard or vegetable plot, these rustic summer houses offer working people a weekend retreat in which to breathe fresh, pure country air. Away from the hubbub, the *dacha* people (*dachniks*) dig, weed, prune and water, enjoying the fruits of their labour at outdoor *shashlyk* parties by lakes and rivers, singing songs and living life at the pace of yesteryear.

Just a decade or so ago, only the few wealthy *dacha* owners had a telephone, hot water and a bathroom in their summerhouse, where camping-style gas stoves and makeshift showers were the norm. Today, the countryside that wraps around the capital is dubbed the Hamptons of Moscow – such is its chichi allure. Turn west down Moscow's noisy ten-lane highway towards Istrinskiy to watch old and new Russia flash by from tower blocks to rustic villages of pretty, wooden tumbledown peasant cottages amongst lush pine forests. Here, weekending *dachniks* tend to their plots of apples, currants, beetroots, cabbages, onions, garlic, berries, pears, plums, potatoes, cucumbers, pumpkins and vines. With their corrugated metal roofs, faded colours and folksy carved decorations, the *dacha* offers a poignant snapshot of pre-revolutionary Russia, surviving revolutions, purges and falls. These homes-away-from-home remain a hard-to-define part of Russian life that the nation holds dear, a return to the soil, to the ways of their forefathers.

068

ST PETERSBURG

CONTACTS
Grand Hotel Europe
Tel: +7 812 94 31 84 9
Email:Yulia.Pashkovskaya@
grandhoteleurope.com
www.grandhoteleurope.com

Ballerina Polina Kutepova
performs at the dazzlingly
romantic Pushkin Golden
Autumn Ball.

There is no Russian who does not know the name of Alexander Pushkin; the country's greatest romantic poet and 19th-century literary pioneer whose name is synonymous with St Petersburg. Created in 1999 as a star-studded Russian-American celebration to honour the 200th anniversary of Pushkin's birth, the now-famous International Pushkin Conference draws over 300 Pushkin Scholars from around the world. The glittering Pushkin Golden Autumn Ball – borne out of Pushkin's poetic adoration for the autumn season – takes place on the outskirts of St Petersburg in Catherine Palace, an important part of Pushkin's biographical jigsaw. It was in this building that the young poet once studied under the auspicious guidance of poet Gavriil Derjavin. His storytelling, poetic style mixes romance, drama and satire with delicate, sensual plots of innocence, passion and love.

Today Pushkin's rich, romantic legacy lives on in this much-awaited annual costumed commemoration, renowned for swirling romance and poetic acclaim. It is an evening of magical splendour in homage to Russia's literary great; a social whirl of silk, velvet, taffeta and pearls. Rastrelli's enormous pastel pink-trimmed, late-Baroque palace, with its seemingly endless rows of gilded atlantes, has some of the most extravagant interiors in Europe. More than 100 kilograms of gold were used to gild the sophisticated stucco façade with its glorious, whipped cream feel and numerous roof-top statues. Bejewelled halls are filled with gilded wall-carvings and ornamental flower-shaped frescoes and inlaid precious woods. Amidst sumptuous silks and velvets, the assembled throng chink glasses to toast to life, love, art and Pushkin in a city where all three collide.

Tickets are snapped up like gold-dust by an elite guest list from the realms of business, politics and culture, from famous actors, poets and musicians to Olympic champions and cabinet ministers. Decked in bejewelled historic opulence and gilded glamour, the Catherine Palace provides the perfect setting for a ball in the style of Alexandra Pushkin's bourgeoisie epoch. Under the Patronage of H.S.H. Prince George Yourievsky, the event is a glitzy affair that begins with tall-stemmed flutes of fine Champagne. Then an elaborate menu unfolds, producing one exquisite course after another, from smoked duck and caviar to an array of fine wines. A stunning collection of gorgeous gowns threaten to eclipse the resplendent palatial decor of the Catherine Palace. Now in its ninth year, the Golden Autumn Ball is a firm fixture in the diaries of St Petersburg's socialites and aristocracy, attracting snapping paparazzi and raising vast sums for charity to boot.

Located at the mouth of the Neva River, on the edge of the Baltic Sea, St Petersburg is a poetic composition of grandiose proportions. Romance, art, passion and spirit seem inextricably entwined within its architecture: a 'living gallery' where visitors drift amongst a striking romantic artistry. Hills, lakes and coastal strips are splashed with the vibrant blues, reds, golds and greens of St Petersburg's vast palaces, cathedrals and castles. Colourful spires, stucco columns, towering domes and ornate gilt work sit above a thread of rivers and canals, earning St Petersburg the title 'The Venice of the North'. With a character quite unlike any other in Russia, the city of St Petersburg's spirited passion is all-encompassing. *Lyubov – iskusstvo i iskusstvo – lyubov*! ('love is art and art is love') the Russian bourgeoisie once exclaimed; the two are unified, both in the city's innumerable galleries and museums and on the streets itself.

Guests at the Pushkin Golden Autumn Ball enjoy a romantic programme redolent of the Pushkin era, from heartfelt operatic fragments based on the great man's works, to ballet and theatre inspired by his life's loves. A limited number of visiting weekenders can join VIPs that include descendants of the Pushkins, the Romanovs and other Russian dynasties at the event. The package, courtesy of the Grand Hotel Europe, costs around 1000 euros per person, staying in a historic suite for three nights, with a carriage (a luxury limousine) and a ticket to the Pushkin Golden Ball as part of the deal.

UKRAINE

TIME DIFFERENCE GMT +1

TELEPHONE CODE +380

CURRENCY Ukranian Hryvnia

LANGUAGE Ukranian, Russian, Romanian

POPULATION 45.9 million

SIZE OF COUNTRY 603,700 sq km
(233,088 sq miles)

CAPITAL Kiev

WHEN TO GO Ukraine is perhaps best known for
its colourful festivals that take place during the
summer months; the best time to visit is between
June and September when the weather is
warmest. Winter can be very cold, particularly in
the mountains, though the Carpathian Mountains
are home to a few great value skiing resorts.

TOURIST INFORMATION
No official national tourist board at present, but try:
www.visit-ukraine.com.ua

Bordered by Russia to the east, Balarus to the north, Poland, Slovia
and Hungary to the west, Romania and Moldova to the southwest
and the Black Sea and Sea of Azov to the south, Ukraine is a land of
broad, fertile agricultural plains. Europe's second largest country rises
to upland areas on the Crimean peninsula and the Carpathian
Mountains. Ukraine's highest point at 2,061 m (6,760 ft) is Mount
Hoverla, its soaring peaks punctuating the west. Marshes and
wooded lowlands characterize the north where pine, oak, beech and
maple thrive in thickets. Kiev and Odessa are two of the largest cities
and boast stone-age ruins, Pan-Mediterranean architecture and
storied histories crossed by rivers that run to the Black Sea.

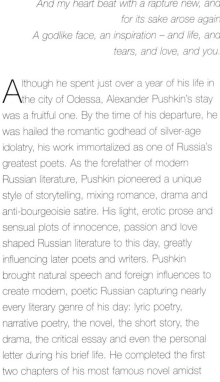

CONTACTS
www.traveltoukraine.org

The Opera House, Odessa.

ODESSA

*And my heart beat with a rapture new, and
for its sake arose again
A godlike face, an inspiration – and life, and
tears, and love, and you.*

Although he spent just over a year of his life in the city of Odessa, Alexander Pushkin's stay was a fruitful one. By the time of his departure, he was hailed the romantic godhead of silver-age idolatry, his work immortalized as one of Russia's greatest poets. As the forefather of modern Russian literature, Pushkin pioneered a unique style of storytelling, mixing romance, drama and anti-bourgeoisie satire. His light, erotic prose and sensual plots of innocence, passion and love shaped Russian literature to this day, greatly influencing later poets and writers. Pushkin brought natural speech and foreign influences to create modern, poetic Russian capturing nearly every literary genre of his day: lyric poetry, narrative poetry, the novel, the short story, the drama, the critical essay and even the personal letter during his brief life. He completed the first two chapters of his most famous novel amidst Odessa's resplendent, ochre-coloured stucco, Renaissance facades and silver domes. In a fitting honour, the city's romantic main street today bears Pushkin's name while city-wide his rich, romantic legacy lives on.

Built in 1898, Odessa's grand Philharmonic Theatre seats a thousand people in opulent style. Designed by Mario Bernardazzi, the famous Odessa architect of Italian origin, the hall is a fine example of turn of the century Venetian-Gothic architecture. As a fertile ground for Russian composers, Pushkin's works have inspired legions of landmark operas, from Glinka's *Ruslan* and *Lyudmila* and Tchaikovsky's *Eugene Onegin* to Mussorgsky's monumental *Boris Godunov*. Pushkin's life and works have also led to innumerable ballets, cantatas and musical scores together with songs set to original verse. Odessa's musical success story is impressive for a post-Soviet nation and the city's thriving arts scene continues to stir great painters, sculptors and artisans. Tales of evocative sunsets on the city's Arcadia Beach are popular literary themes together with entwined passion in leafy Shevchenko Park amidst ornate limestone buildings bathed in sunshine. Bright sun-filled colours, harbour views and warm, open skies continue to evoke the charm of a romantic era on a dazzling backdrop of cobbled streets, tree-hemmed boulevards and Art Nouveau, Renaissance and Neo-classical architecture. Chosen as the setting for some of the most moving and celebrated of Soviet-era films, Odessa continues to be immortalised in film and cinema; its rousing tradition of romance, art and humour define it as a lasting pioneer.

BULGARIA

TIME DIFFERENCE GMT +2

TELEPHONE CODE +359

CURRENCY Lev

LANGUAGE Bulgarian

POPULATION 7.3 million

SIZE OF COUNTRY 110,910 sq km (43,255 sq miles)

CAPITAL Sofia

WHEN TO GO Northern Bulgaria has a moderate continental climate, while southern Bulgaria is distinctly Mediterranean. Summers are hot, winters are cool and crisp, while spring and autumn can be pleasantly mild. Half a dozen mountain ranges play a significant part in determining regional variances, with cold temperatures in the peaks and on the maritime Black Sea coast.

TOURIST INFORMATION
Bulgarian National Tourist Board
Tel: +359 2933 5845
Fax: +359 2989 6939
Email: info@bulgariatravel.org
www.bulgariatravel.org

Occupying the southeastern segment of the Balkan Peninsular, Bulgaria was founded in AD 681, making it Europe's most elderly state. Home to an impressive array of ornate mosques, rustic villages and flamboyantly decorated churches, Bulgaria boasts a rich folkloric tradition on a varied, beautiful and rugged terrain. Fertile valleys give way to the rolling plains of the Danube, with large mountainous areas and coastal lowlands along the Black Sea. Old fishing settlements remain much as they have done for centuries just a stone's throw from the vibrant capital, Sofia, still home to a number of ancient Roman and Byzantine buildings and a UNESCO-protected World Heritage site.

CONTACTS
Bankya Palace Spa
Tel: 02 812 2020
Fax: 02 997 7064
Email: hotel@bankyapalace.com
www.bankyapalace.com

Bankya's verdant hills lie just a short distance from the bustling city of Sofia.

SOFIA

In olden times, the gentry of Sofia sought restorative recuperation in the fresh, pure mountain air and healing waters of Bankya, just 17 km (11 miles) to the west of the city. Back then, it was a full day's travel across thickly tangled wooded terrain riddled with treacherous, pockmarked trails. Today Bankya's lush green valleys and rejuvenating, curative springs are just a 30-minute drive from Sofia's traffic-jammed centre, with a sleek paved road connecting it to the capital door-to-door. As Bulgaria's wellbeing centre, historic Bankya's spa credentials centre on the health-giving virtues of its underground, mineral-rich hypothermal springs. Set in the romantic foothills of the magnificent Lulin Mountain (at 630 m/2,066 ft), the town's temperate, sun-blessed climate has earned it an early reputation for wellness. An unpredictable mountain breeze changes direction in variable gusts to keep the air fresh and pure. In addition, a high concentration of negative ions helps lift mood levels and strengthen positive thought.

Today Bankya is one of Bulgaria's best known and most frequented spa resorts, drawing on the subterranean resources on which it built its foundations with gushing geothermal waters that bubble to temperatures of up to 37°C (99°F) fed by innumerable natural wells. High in hydrocarbon and sodium, this single hydrothermal source of colourless, odour-free water is good enough to bottle – imbibe twice a day, whisper the locals, and you'll be virile and strong with the constitution of an ox.

After Bulgaria's Liberation from Ottoman rule in 1878, a grateful local population donated a scrap of land near the mineral spring to Major Kosta Panitza, a hero from the Battle of Slivnitsa. He built the first hotel in the area, which had about a dozen rooms and the Bulgarian flag flying on its roof – Bankya was in business. Today, the town is home to dozens of well-being centres and spas dedicated to soothing mind, body and soul together with a string of cosy restaurants and bars. Innumerable historic and cultural attractions stem from the age of the Thracian settlers 2,500 years ago and the ruins of a Roman civilization. Explore mountain trails through grassy meadows carpeted in brightly-coloured flowers to fast-flowing sparkling streams and scrub-covered plateaux overlooking giant ravines. Or visit romantic spring-fed pools set in lush, green woodlands amidst the sweet sounds of nature to share in Bankya's blissful serenity, praised for centuries by statesmen, philosophers, poets and scholars.

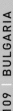

VELIKO TURNOVO

CONTACTS
D&D Tours
Tel: +359 88 8325574 &
+359 2 8277157
Email: ofis@transport-bg.net
www.transport-bg.net

A passerby once marvelled that Veliko Turnovo could "draw poetry from any man", and Bulgaria's picturesque former capital retains considerable romantic beauty. Generations of Bulgarian writers have sought answers and inspiration from the gentle curves of the river that press seductively against the historic ramparts of the town. Above, dozens of charming, varicoloured red-roofed houses teeter on the town's steep slopes "like frightened sheep on rocks", in the words of a 19th century poet. Wedged between a grassy hill and two fast-flowing gorges on the banks of the River Yantra, Veliko Turnovo is hemmed by tiny tree-topped islands and flower-filled shrubberies, and straddled by an iconic landmark bridge. Yet it is the city's handsome fortress, an imposing symbol of Veliko Turnovo's former power, at its very core that draws involuntary gasps of breath, especially after dark when the medieval citadel boasts a softly illuminated glow.

Veliko Turnovo's fortified Tsarevets Castle is bound by a thick stone wall bangle studded with medieval ramparts. The fortified shaft of the Patriarch's Tower stands proud at the centre overlooking Execution Rock to the north, where traitors and invaders were tossed into the Yantra's weed-tangled depths. Shielded by the protective slopes of the storied Turnovo Hills, 240 km (149 miles) northeast of the modern capital, Sofia, Veliko Turnovo boasts Bulgaria's most glorious historical past and symbolizes statehood and national pride in every Bulgarian heart. Settled since the third millennium BC with traces of Thracian civilizations, the town bears the telltale sign of Roman rule in its magnificent palaces, monasteries, churches, bridges, mansions and fortifications. Ancient burial sites around the city were built for some of the nation's early kings, set amidst thick forests and green neo-Byzantine domes. Take time to delve into shady cobbled streets to discover artisans peddling crafts and painting gilt icons outside antique shops piled high with dusty maps and communist-era clutter. Buy armfuls of fresh, sweet-smelling flowers from the Varosha district's streetside florists in Bulgaria's huddled architectural amphitheatre, once partially destroyed by Ottoman rule but now restored and resplendent. Veliko Turnovo represents a romantic symbolic bastion of national Bulgarian grit, camaraderie and spirit with flags unfurled atop romantic towers and aged stately spires.

The beautiful streets of Veliko Turnoko have inspired poets and romantics alike for centuries.

ROMANIA

Over a third of Romania's fish-shaped landmass is shrouded in thick forest, with the Carpathian Mountains, peaking at Mount Moldoveanu at 2,544 m (8,344 ft), running from the north to the southwest. 10,000-year-old glacial lakes, volcanic rocks and boggy marshes are dominant landscape features with castles, orchards and vineyards in the foothills of undulating spines. The Danube delta's reed bed sediment provides rich nourishment to fish-filled rivers. Folkloric Transylvania – home to Bran Castle of Dracula fame – is one of Romania's most beautiful regions, while Bucharest's Belle Époque mansions and tree-lined boulevards have earned it the nickname 'Little Paris'.

TIME DIFFERENCE GMT +2

TELEPHONE CODE +40

CURRENCY Leu

LANGUAGE Romanian

POPULATION 22.2 million

SIZE OF COUNTRY 238,391 sq km (92,972 sq miles)

CAPITAL Bucharest

WHEN TO GO Scorching summer highs form a sharp contrast with cold snowy winters from mid-December until the end of March. June, July and August are hottest near the Black Sea coast, where average temperatures reach 24–30°C (75–86°F). In summer there are frequent showers and thunderstorms in the mountains. Pleasant autumn days keep the sunshine going until mid-October, but Transylvania and the Carpathian Mountains can be wet year-round.

TOURIST INFORMATION
Romania National Tourist Office
Tel: 020 7224 3692
Email: romaniatravel@btconnect.com
www.romaniatourism.com

CONTACTS
Casa Vernescu
Tel: +40 213 11 44
Fax: +40 212 12 54 87
Email: office@casavernescu.ro
www.casavernescu.ro

Best Limousine Romania
Tel: +40 495 92 14 51 0
Email: info@bestlimo.ru
www.bestlimousine.ro

Take a limousine tour through Bucharest's wide boulevards, steeped in history.

BUCHAREST

Romania's national bard, Mihai Eminescu, described his homeland as "a true poetic maze" and this storied land of myths, folklore, kings and fairies evokes a mysterious, legend-steeped charm. A host of well-preserved medieval spires, castles, winding rivers, vast chateaus, wondrous cathedrals and beautifully painted monasteries, wrapped in sunflower meadows and tumbling vines, beg to be discovered. Dubbed 'Little Paris' by European aristocrats, Bucharest is characterized by wide, tree-lined boulevards, Belle Époque facades, ornate balconies, huge palaces and faded frescoes rich in royal intrigues and heartfelt love.

It is possible to discover some of this fine, romantic, regal history in Bucharest's treasure-filled palaces, ancient monuments and noble courts, although sadly a horse-drawn carriage isn't an option – yet. Instead, hire a chauffeur-driven luxury limousine (complete, on request, with a bottle of chilled, sparkling Romanian Muscat). Settle into leather seats for a voyage through Bucharest's romantic splendour to royal jewels and the gold- and gem-studded history of Romania to the Old Court of the past and the vestiges of the former princely palaces. Marvel at the Palace of the Parliament, the second-largest building on the planet after the Pentagon in America, before

crawling along the pretty, balconied streets to Curtea de Arges, where Prince Neagoe Basarab built a glorious monastery amidst magnificent Neo-classical fountains and Gothic spires.

Glide along tree-hemmed Kiseleff Boulevard to the atmospheric grandeur of the intersection with Marshal Prezan and Marshal Averescu Boulevards, near leafy Herastrau Park. The statuesque Arch of Triumph, designed by Petre Antonescu, dominates the streetscape, with its heraldic medallions, royal crowns and sculptures. Ask your driver to circle at close quarters for the best views. Wind down the window to glimpse plaques that honour military endeavour and the 1918 Union of Romanian provinces.

Join the synchronized flow of traffic, past grand towers and formidable gatehouses for a kerbside view of flag-topped Cotroceni Palace. The building is now a presidential residence and museum that houses the Romanian royal family's collections. Tours explore prolific art and a wealth of historical documents that narrate the romantic sagas of Romania's kings and queens.

Ask your chauffeur to drop you at the opulent Casa Vernescu for fine dining in rich 19th-century opulence. Choose from luxurious dishes, surrounded by marble columns and gilded mirrors that evoke the historic chronicles of eras past.

HUNGARY

A complex fusion of Balkan and Slavic influences add to the Hungarian national mix – a historic melting pot of Finno-Ugric and Turkish invasion that shares borders with Slovakia, Ukraine, Romania, Croatia, Serbia, Austria and Slovenia. Hungary's thousands of acres of vineyards and orchards, plus hundreds of nature reserves and national parks, are complemented by some stunning stretches of water, such as fish-filled Lake Balaton. Much of Hungary's landscape bubbles with hot, thermal subterranean springs – the source of dozens of medicinal baths and curative spas. Lively Budapest boasts a dynamic literary and arts scene on a beautiful stretch of the Danube dotted with floating restaurants and pleasure craft.

TIME DIFFERENCE GMT +1

TELEPHONE CODE +36

CURRENCY Forint

LANGUAGE Hungarian

POPULATION 9.9 million

SIZE OF COUNTRY 92,340 sq km (36,013 sq miles)

CAPITAL Budapest

WHEN TO GO Hungary is characterized by warm, dry summers and fairly cold winters, with January the coldest month. May to September is mild and pleasant, with cool nights and comfortable daytime temperatures. October to December is chilly and wet and sometimes snowy. January and February are usually subject to snowfall, especially in the mountainous regions.

TOURIST INFORMATION
Hungarian Tourist Board
Tel: 020 7823 0412
Email: info@gotohungary.co.uk
www.gotohungary.co.uk

073

BUDAPEST

CONTACTS
BAV Jewellery (Rubin Ékszerbolt)
V. Párizsi utca 2
Tel: +36 318 62 17
www.bav.hu
Open Mon–Fri 10–6, Sat 10–1

Translator Team (Antiques)
Tel: +36 309 82 62 86
Fax: +36 126 08 33 9
Email: sales@TranslatorTeam.com
www.translatorteam.com

*Budapest is the perfect place
to pick out unique treasures for
a loved-one.*

Few gifts say 'I love you' like a hand-picked trinket to cherish. A one-of-a-kind present chosen with care demonstrates consideration and forethought. It also exhibits an ability to go beyond the norm when it comes to gift-giving rather than relying on well-worn clichés. For a romantic gesture, Budapest's backstreet flea markets and musty antique shops offer a fine array of knick-knacks and collectables, from bejewelled bric-a-brac and historic artworks to the downright bizarre. Unlike the French and Italian aristocracy, Budapest's Austro-Hungarian bourgeoisie didn't come into their own until the late 1800s, by which time these newly affluent upper classes were determined to make up for lost time. They indulged every whim, filling their expansive homes with commissioned art, jewellery and furnishings in a golden era of Neo-classical, Renaissance and Art Deco style. However, almost 50 years of Soviet occupation brought lean times in the 1990s, prompting the great-grandchildren of those affluent aristocrats to begin selling off the family treasures for cash. Today, the city is a dazzling treasure trove of Hungarian curios – dubbed the Paris of the East for its eye-popping array of handsome antiques – you simply need to know where to look.

Budapest's 50 antique stores and funky junk stalls are clustered together in two separate rows of shop-frontages displaying an eclectic mishmash of timepieces, porcelain dolls, gold, silver and glass. The city's more upmarket 'Antique Row' near the capital's parliament is housed in a string of spruced-up old buildings where cupboard-sized Aladdin's Caves piled high with boxes of forgotten memories offer barely enough room for one customer. Below ground, a succession of cavernous vaults contain enough riches to furnish a royal palace, such as silver jewellery, paintings, furniture, rugs and Oriental arts. Hidden doors lead to Budapest's most famous auction houses, while upstairs attic rooms hide one-off pieces of art and quirky collectables from an oeuvre of obscure artists. Tea-coloured documents, dog-eared charts and maps adorn the walls together with framed numismatic items and letters in ancient script.

The Ecseri Flea Market (*Piac*) is an altogether more ramshackle affair in the southeastern part of the city, near the Ecseri út Metro 3 stop. Budapest's biggest second-hand market offers browsers a staggering array of trash and treasure, from classic art to kitsch. Every object has a tale to tell, be it old or new, amidst the vendors and hustle and bustle. Haggle for a bargain – it's an expected part of the deal – be it an authentic 18th-century cigarette box or kooky costume pendant.

To unearth all manner of old curiosities it pays to rummage amidst the socialist-era pamphlets, fossils and souvenir jumble at the flea markets. Uncover nostalgic mementoes of a Hungarian yesterday in Budapest's dusty trinket dens, from old postcards to faded prints of a favourite city with romantic memories. Pick amongst the clutter to discover that perfect silver ring box, or hunt out an antique photo frame in which to place a treasured snap. Looking for a dream ring? Budapest's mysterious side-street stores offer enchanting antique jewellery from glittering 19th-century treasures to golden bands of the past. But hold off doling out big bucks unless you really know your Zsolnay from your tat – or have an antiques expert in tow.

A number of bilingual antiques specialists fluent in Hungarian 'antiquese' offer guided tours around Budapest's prime haunts to seek out rarities or perfect gifts. Expect to pay around 250 euros for a full day packed full of tips and practical advice from a local, in-the-know expert – including how to barter over price. Your guide will be fully familiar with current Hungarian Customs and VAT refund regulations in Hungary (as well as shipping arrangements) and will know their way around Budapest's antique auctions and catalogues.

Shoppers keen to track down a truly individual, romantic gift will find plenty of highlights at BAV Jewellery on V. Párizsi utca; a state-owned antiques chain that stocks lots of fine old watches and antique jewellery, and where gold and silver rings, brooches and necklaces can often be snapped up for a song.

PUSZTA

CONTACTS
Hungarian National Tourist Office
Tel: +44 (0)20 7823 1032
www.hungarytourism.hu

Details of horse-riding events are
available from the Hungarian
Equestrian Tourist Association
(www.equi.hu/eng).

*The vast, poppy-studded
Hungarian Great Plains
are romantic in their
breathtaking isolation.*

While the romantic element may be disappearing from modern life in Hungary, the poetic state remains keenly observed on the rolling grasslands of the Great Hungarian Plain. Stretching from the Danube to the country's eastern border to form an expansive prairie the size of Holland, the *puszta* (meaning empty, bare, grassy plain) has captivated generations of painters and poets, as exemplified by Hungary's great 19th-century romantic poet, Sandor Petofi, who described daybreak on the plain thus: "When the sun rose, dismissing the moon with its motion...flat as an ocean...stretched for ever, unending." Traditional courtship songs remain intrinsic to the traditions of the plains-folk who live in romantic isolation amidst treeless carpets of sun-parched wheat stubble. Nothing breaks the terrain's flatness apart from a few scrappy juniper bushes bathed in sunlight on an undulating crest. Around crackling open fires, these wandering people sing a heartfelt lament of homesickness and age-old yearning, surrounded by cattle from a thousand hills. A zillion dust-churned hoof-prints encircle sporadic tufts of beech and acacia under the gauzy moon of a silent sky.

Only the brave or the foolhardy would entertain the idea of exploring these great plains without local insight, as mile upon mile of unmarked tracks are completely baffling to a stranger. Much like the vast Argentine pampas, Hungary's whip-cracking

cowboy country is synonymous with cattle-driving, horsemanship and magnificent sunrises across the savannas. In the plains, a fierce code of independence epitomizes the spiritual embodiment of the Hungarian nation, much like the cowboy symbolizes American grit. Horses still graze loose across the plains to the sound of lowing oxen and tinkling cattle bells. The snare-drum roll of hooves and the snapping whip of the *csikós* (tribes) resonates throughout every aspect of pastoral life, steeped in old-time traditions and spirit. Lasso love-duels remain common in prairie life in the fierce summer sun, when a sure eye and a steady hand decide who will love – and who will lose.

The vast Great Hungarian Plain has the most extreme weather of any area in Hungary, with searing heat during the long, hot summers and bleak, cold winter months. Yet these alkaline, scrubby lowlands remain unchanged by time, evoking a romantic era of the Hungarian *puszta* of eras past. Hungarian grey cattle, stud horses, Racka sheep with spiral-shaped horns and buffalo herds graze on open pastures. Hungary's Nonius horse breeds are reared here as they have been for three centuries on a raw, harsh landscape, just a couple of hours from Budapest yet half a world away.

Numerous tour companies run full-day forays to the Great Hungarian Plains, where visitors can journey the grasslands in a traditional wooden *vardo* (horse-drawn cart). Enjoy a welcome drink of *barack pálinka* (apricot schnapps) served with the *puszta*'s customary *pogácsa* (salty scone) before meeting the region's legendary horsemen. Skill in the saddle defines status here, the difference between conquest and defeat in the warriors of a bygone age. Today, descendants perform insane feats of showmanship for visitors, riding bareback at breakneck speed in ever-decreasing circles or driving teams of a dozen horses standing with one foot planted on the hindquarters of the rear pair. With whips popping like revolvers and wide-legged trousers flapping in the wind, riders pull their hats down low to steer horses in a fast-moving stream.

Hungary's flat, rolling expanses are also journeyed by horse-drawn wooden wagons and the people of the plains have developed some of the finest harness systems and cart designs on the planet. Today, these horse-drawn wagons remain crucial to the nomadic, pastoral plains-folk traversing the settlements of this dusty, bump-ridden terrain. Visit from March to April for the best of the weather in this exposed landscape, and budget for around 75 euros per person, including a free pick-up from most Budapest city centre hotels. Cosy up on sheepskin-covered seats for a romantic voyage across the unspoiled domain of skulking prairie dogs before savouring a lunch of goulash from a stew-pot kettle simmering over an open fire, accompanied by the romantic strains of fiddle-led Hungarian gipsy music.

SLOVENIA

TIME DIFFERENCE GMT +1

TELEPHONE CODE +386

CURRENCY Euro

LANGUAGE Slovene

POPULATION 2 million

SIZE OF COUNTRY 20,273 sq km
(7,906 sq miles)

CAPITAL Ljubljana

WHEN TO GO Slovenia's varied climate includes
a continental weather pattern in the northeast, a
harsh Alpine climate in the mountains and a sub-
Mediterranean climate on the coast. For walkers
and hikers, April–June offers a colourful wildflower
landscape as well as inexpensive prices. Both are
gone by the time a dry, hot summer arrives, while
pleasant autumns can often bring fog and snow
by mid-October.

TOURIST INFORMATION
Embassy of the Republic of Slovenia
Tel: 020 7222 5400
Fax: 020 7222 5277
Email: vlo@gov.si
www.slovenia.info

Slovenia sits tucked between Italy, Austria, Hungary and Croatia in a
small pocket of heavily wooded terrain looped by meadows, lakes,
rivers and historic towns. A limestone region of subterranean
streams, caves, and gorges occupies the stretch between Ljubljana,
the capital, and the Adriatic coast. Likened to a miniature Prague
without the tourist crowds, Ljubljana offers easy access to Triglav
National Park – a vast, mountainous expanse that spans the major
part of the Julian Alps. Rolling savannahs stretch out towards Croatia
and Hungary while romantic castles and vine-clad terraces
predominate to the west.

CONTACTS
Wine Cellar Goriska Brda
Tel. +386 53 31 01 44
Email: tourism@klet-brda.si
www.klet-brda.com

Raise a glass to your beloved in the picturesque vineyards around Bohinj.

BOHINJ

It is said that Slovenia has two great loves: words and wine, with both commonly intertwined throughout a history rich in literature and viniculture. Hailing their unique language as the perfect lovebird communiqué, Slovenes speak a rare, modern, dual-aspect dialect that has retained a double grammatical form, earning it a romantic charm. Slovenia is also the only country in the world with the word 'love' in it, as a flick through an atlas will bear out. In the hilly wine-growing region of Goriska Brda, the vine-fringed village of Medana plays host to poets and wine connoisseurs in August each year. With glasses raised to the heavens under the thick boughs of an ancient mulberry tree, recitals and quaffing sessions toast bards, burlesques, ballads and bouquet alike.

Slovenia's passion for poetry and wine manifests itself in festivals and celebrations across the country's western flank. Regional anthologies of verse draw on the centuries-old Slovene tradition of winegrowing and its literary arts. Archaeological finds over the years indicate that both were present in Slovenia's aged cultures, almost certainly a legacy of the ancient Greeks. Under the Romans, viniculture and the wonder of words began to truly blossom as subsequent excavations of amphorae, goblets, earthenware wine jugs and Latin script bear out. Growers spiced their full-bodied vintages with lemon peel, wormwood, pepper and sage during the golden age of Roman literature. Winegrowing almost died out in the 6th century AD when the first migrant Slavs settled in the area, under threat from Hungarian tribes, but returned with the Christianization of the region. Each monastery established a vineyard (*vinograd*) as did Slovenia's landed aristocracy and emerging bourgeoisie. Today, Slovenia produces over 20 million gallons of wine annually from some 21,600 hectares of vines. A crossroads between north and south, east and west, travellers continue to bring viniculture knowledge to Slovenia from other wine-growing nations, resulting in a French-, Italian-, and German-influenced melting pot that is mirrored in the nation's literary arts. Stroll through the arched cellars and abundant grape crops of the Wine Cellar Goriska Brda (2.50 euros per person) to debate the merits of the Rebula Quercus over an earthy Merlot Bagueri. Then engage in 'Poetry To Make Wine Sweeter' at the birthplace of poet Alojz Gradnik, a scribe who elevated the language of the Slovene peasants to a written art form, conveying themes of erotic passion and the romantic sentiments of pain and hope.

CROATIA

TIME DIFFERENCE GMT +1

TELEPHONE CODE +385

CURRENCY Kuna

LANGUAGE Croatian

POPULATION 4.49 million

SIZE OF COUNTRY 56,542 sq km
(22,051 sq miles)

CAPITAL Zagreb

WHEN TO GO Pleasant, mild temperatures in
April and September are spared the humidity of
Croatia's oppressive summer highs. May and
June boast long, sunny days. By October, the
weather is too cool for camping but still suitable
for outdoor pursuits. By early November, the cold
has set in – as has the wind and rain.

TOURIST INFORMATION
Croatian National Tourist Office
Tel: 020 8563 7979
Fax: 020 8563 2616
Email: info@croatia-london.co.uk
www.croatia.hr

Sitting adjacent to Italy across the Adriatic in the northern
Mediterranean, Croatia boasts nearly 2000 km (1,240 miles) of rocky,
indented shoreline sprinkled with over a thousand islands – one of
Europe's most dramatic coastal stretches. Numerous off-the-beaten-
track coves and sleepy, stone-built fishing villages remain unspoilt by
modern development, with red-roofed coastal cities packed with
historical Mediterranean culture and ancient remains. Lakes,
mountains and bird-rich marshlands offer vast scope for hikers,
walkers and cyclists. Idyllic wind-funnelled sailing waters lap forested
islets. Curved, sun-drenched bays snake around jagged white cliffs
and sheltered pools offer scuba and snorkelling sites dotted with
caves and wrecks.

DUBROVNIK

Dubrovnik's astonishing, medieval fairytale beauty has captured the hearts of artisans for centuries, but exactly when its so-called lovers' corner was created nobody rightly knows. Immortalized in the aged songs of the troubadours, Porporela is a fine old pier in the base of the fortress of St Ivan. Built to protect the harbour, this formidable breakwater is now synonymous with starlit romantic strolls and offers sheltered sanctuary to lovers seeking momentary refuge, a stolen kiss or romantic tryst. A path from the Old Town, dubbed 'the lovers walk' by locals, snakes through this fair city of angel-white stone to Porporela where legends, steeped in salacious tales of seduction and sweet stories of young love, prevail.

Porporela's robust might helps to shield Dubrovnik old town from the ravages of the sea, as it juts into the deep, clear waters of the Adriatic. Now beautifully restored to its pre-war glory, Dubrovnik bears few scars from the conflict of the 1990s. Girdled by broad stone ramparts and neatly partitioned by the marble-paved central *stradun* (high street), Dubrovnik's handsome harbourside boasts dozens of small family-run seafood restaurants and cosy bars tucked away from the main drag. Amidst the chattering of the street market and muted laughter from tiny upper-storey windows, Dubrovnik's red-tiled roofs, white stone façades and green-blue sea have inspired the palettes of artists from all corners of the globe.

The city's expansive walls are made to be walked, reaching 6 m (19 ft) in width and 25 m (82 ft) in height and studded by towers, fortifications and bastions. Over 700 years of architecture is contained within these ramparts, from a 17th-century Baroque church and pre-Romanesque spire to numerous fine structures from the Gothic and Renaissance eras. From here, Dubrovnik's Lovers' Walk winds down to the water, accompanied by a salty sea breeze infused with the fragrances of wisteria, oleander and cypress. A bell, horn or whistle denotes an arrival in a harbour scattered with sea-facing painters daubing at canvasses to a cacophony of screeching gulls. Embracing couples and lovers reunited enjoy spell-binding views out to Lokrum Island, framed by Dubrovnik's vibrant coastal hues. Mario Nardeli sang: *I will await you, little one, by the red lantern* – a direct reference to Porporela's harbour-mouth crimson beacon. Little wonder that a cosy 'love seat' set in the pier's ancient walls ranks amongst the most popular betrothal spots in Croatia.

CONTACTS
Dubrovnik Tourism Board
Tel: +44 20 323 887 / 323 889
Fax: +44 20 323 725
Email: info@tzdubrovnik.hr
www.tzdubrovnik.hr

Dubrovnik Private Tours
Tel: +385 959 06 06 06
Email: dubrovniktours@gmail.com
www.dubrovnik-tours.info

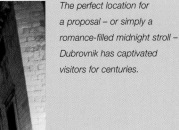

The perfect location for a proposal – or simply a romance-filled midnight stroll – Dubrovnik has captivated visitors for centuries.

CONTACTS
General Turist Ltd (Croatia
Lighthouses)
Tel: +385 14 805 652
Email: Info@generalturist.com
www.generalturist.com

Split Tourism Office
Tel: +385 21 345 606
Fax: +385 21 339 898
Email: tic-split@st.t-com.hr
www.visitsplit.com

*Enjoy secluded romance to the
soothing sounds of the sea.*

SPLIT

For generations, Croatia's nautical splendour was purely the domain of seafarers and fishermen who navigated the wave-lapped Adriatic coast's islands, bays and beaches. Since ancient times, the region's rugged coves and perilous, jagged spits have challenged even the most skilful of mariners. To guide their men safely homeward, the women set huge beacons ablaze along the Adriatic shore, igniting coals in iron baskets hung from sharp-ended poles. They also called upon the protective powers of the water maid, a mythical figure believed to provide safe shelter to seafarers in stormy waters. Over time, stone-built lighthouses replaced the bonfires that raged along the coast. Acting as a marker by day and projecting beams of light by night, each lighthouse is erected at a strategic point on a rocky shoreline ledge, island, reef or cliff – a beacon of hope lashed by sea-spray and crashing waves.

Today, Croatia's lighthouse tradition has been immortalized in a thousand respected books and galleries, including a 2006 sell-out photographic exhibition in Vienna. Hundreds remain in working order after many years of loyal service, with even the smallest beacon often offering living quarters for a lighthouse keeper. Others have been adapted to use automated electric lights that no longer require a full-time resident operator. All boast breathtaking views across atolls, coves and open water with many, such as the Sv Petar lighthouse, rentable by tourists seeking the ultimate coastal bolthole. Built in 1884 on a rock-strewn cape, the pepper pot-shaped structure rises up triumphantly from the shale-hemmed sea and gorgeous beaches. Smooth, flat rocks offer suntraps and tanning ledges amidst the natural splendour of wooded parklands, complete with bird-filled trails. An expansive rock-built terrace offers unforgettable coastal vistas where shellfish suppers can be enjoyed at sunrise serenaded by the lulling sounds of the sea. Cosy, uninterrupted romance is assured in this unique coastal retreat; the radiating beams are fully automated, so there will be no poorly timed intrusion from the lighthouse keeper. There is, however, a housekeeper for guests happy to forgo the dusting for more romantic pursuits.

SERBIA

Landlocked Serbia spans the southern Pannonian Plains and central Balkan region, bordered by Hungary to the north, Romania and Bulgaria to the east, Macedonia and Albania to the south and Croatia, Bosnia-Herzegovina and Montenegro to the west. Limestone cave systems, wetlands, lava-formed pyramids, blooming meadows and fine old settlements characterize the Serbian countryside, while capital Belgrade continues to be shaped by its history, both past and present. Conquered and rebuilt by Celts, Romans, Slavs, Turks and Austro-Hungarians, Belgrade is dominated by the mighty Kalemegdan Fortress at the confluence of the Danube and Sava rivers.

TIME DIFFERENCE GMT +1

TELEPHONE CODE +381

CURRENCY Dinar

LANGUAGE Serbian, Hungarian

POPULATION 10.16 million

SIZE OF COUNTRY 77,474 sq km (29,912 sq miles)

CAPITAL Belgrade

WHEN TO GO Serbia enjoys a typical Mediterranean climate of mild winters and hot, dry summers, with highest temperatures in the central provinces and the coolest regions in the highlands. The average mid-summer temperature is 24°C (75°F) degrees.

TOURIST INFORMATION
National Tourism Organization of Serbia
Tel: + 381 11 32 32 586
Fax: + 381 11 32 21 068
Email: office@serbia.travel
www.serbia-tourism.org

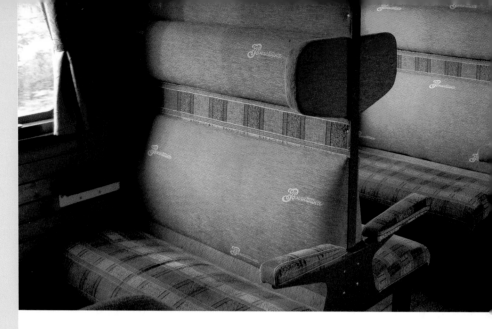

CONTACTS
Steam Train Romantika
Tel. +381 113 61 69 28
Email: romantika@yurail.co.yu
www.yurail.co.yu

The faded glamour of the Romantika's interiors suggest old-world romance.

BELGRADE

It runs infrequently, advertises sporadically and follows a route shrouded in mystery, yet Serbia's romantic steam train embodies the very spirit of the classic era of travel. Those lucky enough to board Serbia's only steam-hauled locomotive are in for an unforgettable day-long voyage. From your historic carriage, leave the old clay houses, neo-classical spires and futuristic towers of Belgrade (Beograd) behind to the sound of the engine's whistle and the sight of smoke drifting past the windows in billowing clouds. Hugging the track along the banks of the River Danube, bells clanging at each hill tunnel, bridge and historic settlement, the vintage locomotive *Romantika* chugs across some of the most stunning countryside in Serbia. Revel in the authentic, slow-paced glamour of this steam-powered journey as the high drama of a bygone age unfolds.

The *Romantika* is a fine-looking, if slightly worn, 19th-century class 33 locomotive, black and red and emblazoned with a heraldic motif in Cyrillic and Latin scripts. Choose from renovated wood-panelled first-, second- or third-class carriages – the difference being sun-faded upholstery rather than hard, wooden seats – to voyage from the capital to the ancient towns of Sremski Karlovci, Novi Sad and Smederevo. As Serbia's premier preserved standard-gauge, steam-hauled railway, the *Romantika* signifies

considerable nostalgia and excitement *en route* as it journeys back in time. Operating on weekends from late May to September, Serbia's famous historical steam engine transports passengers across the Sava River, a tributary of the Danube, through the gypsy villages and Communist-era apartment blocks of Belgrade's outer suburbs to flat, rolling grassy expanses and fields of vines, corn, oats and wheat. Crimson poppies poke their bright heads from tangled hedgerows amidst meadows of hoeing farmhands, decrepit tractors and grazing cattle.

Romantika's leisurely incursion into Serbia's countryside, first settled in Roman times, allows opportunities to disembark the train to stroll around historic wine-making settlements, Austro-Hungarian towns and storied lands steeped in legends of the Turkish Empire. Visit markets for local wine, crafts, baked goods, honey and plants in brilliant hues, or enjoy fresh peach juice in tree-shaded tranquility under marble fountains, flower-filled balconies and brightly-coloured Baroque spires. Meander through plazas filled with the romantic sounds of accordion music, tolling church bells and twittering birdsong.

Expect to pay between Serbia Dinar 370–1,460 per return ticket from Belgrade Railway Station – departure dates vary so check on the schedule at desk number ten.

MONTENEGRO

Located in the southern part of the Balkan Peninsula, Montenegro is bordered to the west, north and east by Croatia, Bosnia-Herzegovina, Serbia and Kosovo. Albania lies to the south. With over 200 km (124 miles) of Adriatic coastline, Montenegro boasts a strong maritime heritage. Boka Kotorska (the Bay of Boka) is one of the Mediterranean's more romantic harbour-front settings, while hundreds of charming stone-built fishing villages string along the shore. An inland terrain is characterized by high and extensive mountain massifs intersected by gushing river gorges and deep-set valleys, while grassy lowland plains cover the south.

TIME DIFFERENCE GMT +1

TELEPHONE CODE +382

CURRENCY Euro (although Montenegro is outside the euro zone)

LANGUAGE Serbian, Montenegrin

POPULATION 678,177

SIZE OF COUNTRY 13,812 sq km (5,332 sq miles)

CAPITAL Podgorica

WHEN TO GO Hot, dry summers and mild, wet winters characterize Montenegro's Mediterranean coastal climate. In the central plains, temperatures can hit the upper 30°Cs (100°F+), with typical midsummer temperatures averaging 25°C (77°F). Highland regions are cooler, with snowfall throughout the winter months.

TOURIST INFORMATION
Montenegro Tourist Board
Email: info@visit-montenegro.com
www.visit-montenegro.com

079

KOTOR

GETTING THERE
The nearest airport is Tivat, 10 mins from Kotor. Flights from Dubrovnik take 1hr 15mins. On arrival, there is an excellent local bus service.

CONTACTS
www.visit-montenegro.com

View of Saint Nikola Church above the village of Perast on Kotor Bay.

In the 19th century, Lord Byron visited this small coastal town and indulged in a romantic tryst with a local noblewoman. One of the most famous romantic British poets, Byron was one of many visitors taken by Kotor's spectacular scenery, gushing: 'At the moment of birth of our planet, the most beautiful meeting of land and sea was on the Montenegrin coast'. He isn't the only dashing, silver-tongued romantic hero to marvel at Montenegro's pretty cream stone villages, rugged grey-green mountains and calm turquoise sea – a visit by James Bond for the filming of *Casino Royale* sent the country's cachet into stratospheric meltdown as the big-screen brought Montenegro to the world.

Montenegro's romantic heartland is centred on Kotor, a fine UNESCO-status medieval walled town containing a riddle of old narrow streets. One cosy bar and restaurant leads to another amongst monuments, churches and 2,000-year-old cobbled alleys. Kotor's ageing architectural treasure trove spanning the 12th–20th century stretches out to a horseshoe-shaped bay overlooking two distant islands, Sveti Djordje (St George) and Gospa od Skrpijela (Lady of the Rocks). First settled in Roman times, Kotor is surrounded by the mementoes of a rich and colourful history, from ancient burial mounds of 3rd–century BC Illyrian civilization and Hellenic-age ruins to the remains of an Episcopal basilica.

To walk around Kotor's old quarter (Stari Grad) is to discover the town's romantic spirit in the Cathedral of Saint Tryphon, the charming church of St. Ana, Orthodox Church of St Nicolas and the 15th century chapel of St Mary. Witness monumental frescoes, gothic façades, marble-work and ornate altars together with the remnants of a Benedictine monastery from the 7th century amongst once-opulent palaces. Stroll around Kotor Bay, where several broad gulfs morph with narrow sea channels to form one of Europe's finest natural ports. In the foothills of the Lovcen Mountains, discover lemon trees, oranges groves and wild-growing mimosa, camellia, oleander, jasmine and magnolia amongst palms, olives and figs. Grab a cosy two-person table at family-run restaurant Le Bastion (open daily 11am–1am) in the stone-paved old town for romantic dining with authentic Montenegrin charm. Order a glass of grappa and ask about the daily fish specials whilst soaking up the medieval-era ambience from a flower-decked terrace.

GREECE

As the birthplace of European civilization, Greece remains a hotbed of magnificent architecture, sculpture, drama, philosophy and literature and boasts an extraordinary history rich in battles for supremacy. Telltale mementoes of a glorious era provide a captivating historical narrative, from ancient temples and magnificent amphitheatres to civilizations dating back thousands of years. A rugged, dry and dusty interior is home to rustic, whitewashed villages, pebbled alleys, olive groves and citrus trees. In the Aegean Sea, a seemingly endless lacework of coastline is scattered with wave-lapped isles. Capital city Athens remains a centre of learning, while Thessaloniki in the north has a distinctly Byzantine feel. As home to the gods of Greek mythology, snow-frosted Mount Olympus is Greece's highest point at 2,197 m (7,206 ft).

TIME DIFFERENCE GMT +2

TELEPHONE CODE +30

CURRENCY Euro

LANGUAGE Greek

POPULATION 10.7 million

SIZE OF COUNTRY 131,945 sq km
(51,459 sq miles)

CAPITAL Athens

WHEN TO GO A Mediterranean climate boasts plenty of sunshine and a limited amount of rainfall. Dry, hot days in summer are cooled by seasonal winds (*meltemi*) but can still be stifling. Winters are generally mild in lowland areas, with a minimum amount of snow and ice.

TOURIST INFORMATION
Greek National Tourist Office
Tel: 020 7495 9300
Fax: 020 7495 4057
Email: info@gnto.co.uk
www.gnto.co.uk

ATHENS

CONTACTS
Cine Paris
Tel: +30 210 32 22 071 /
+30 210 32 48 057

Athens Tourism
Tel: +30 210 32 53 123
Fax: +30 210 32 16 653
Email: info@atedco.gr
www.athenstourism.gr

At twilight, the aged city of Athens yields to the dramatic illumination of the moon as shifting shadows cast their spell across the pillars of the Acropolis. Soaring columns, mammoth archways and crumbling monuments dominate the cityscape – a distinguished architectural anthology on an epic scale. Neo-classical, Byzantine, Medieval and Hellenic towers represent the vestiges of some of the most enduring historical landmarks on earth, from the majestic Erechtheion and the winged gargoyles of the ornate Temple of Olympian Zeus to the resplendent Temple of Nike. After dark, Athens discovers fresh verve as the city's night owls spill out on to cobbled plazas under the basking amber glow of dim streetlights. On one of the world's most romantic backdrops, more than 100 outdoor cinemas swish open their curtains in the warm night air. Few movie-going experiences compare to this fine Athenian cinematic tradition where motion pictures entertain the crowds amidst jasmine and bougainvillea in the city's leafy parks and backstreet gardens. Moonlit terraces also double as rooftop movie theatres providing atmospheric screenings high above Athens' floodlit hustle and bustle.

Movie-watching (*kinema*) al fresco debuted in Greece in the 19th century when short clips and newscasts were broadcast at dusk. A Golden Era of cinema followed, reflecting a rebirth of the Greek spirit after the tragedies of the Second World War and the Greek Civil War. Athens wanted to get on with enjoying life again and sought laughter, love and triumph in its cinema. Simple projectors were erected across the city just as the sunlight had faded enough to enable the picture to be seen. Today, the films range from homespun vernacular melodramas to big-budget Hollywood spectacles with the occasional 1950's cinematic retrospective thrown in for good measure – digitally re-mastered of course. Vintage romance ignites the teasing suggestion of passion to light a fire in the audience in the genre of classic black and white drama, rare silent films and slush-and-trash B-movies. Cinema turns fancies into love and hopeless dreams into romantic fantasies with *Pillow Talk* (starring Rock Hudson and Doris Day), *The Tender Trap* (Debbie Reynolds and Frank Sinatra) and *Gentlemen Prefer Blondes* (Marilyn Monroe and Jane Russell): the perfect love-bird flicks. Old black and white movies may lack the sophistication of the quick cuts and special effects of modern romantic epics, but the spellbinding magic and tension they engender in an audience is palpable. Even now, more than six decades after its original release, *It Happened One Night* (featuring Clark Gable and Claudette Colbert) provides a near-perfect blend of romantic wit and sentimental charm. With its masterful camera work, this little-heralded gem deservedly swept the top five awards at the 1934 Academy Awards. Though slightly grainy and a

little bit jumpy today, the movie more than stands the test of time – a genuine Hollywood romantic classic. Hailed as the originator of the popular boy-meets-girl scenario, *It Happened One Night* set a high standard for other quirky love stories.

Pack a bean-bag, cushion or blanket (just in case the best seat in the house is on bare ground) and arm yourself with snacks and goodies before snuggling down before the screen. Don't expect Multiplex-style gloss and glamour: Athens is all about the romance of cinema, from the clatter of vintage spooling to show-stopping power outages and tangled tape. Amenities are sparse with just a movie screen, projector and a collection of mismatched lawn chairs together with a stall selling roasted nuts, sunflower seeds, popcorn, beer, liquor and wine. For 9 Euros, a celluloid feast offers movie-goers some delectable surprises be it a subtitled trailer from a bygone movie age or the latest weepy. Nuzzle under a star-scattered sky while catching a flick at Aigli (the oldest outdoor cinema in Athens) or climb up ramshackle stairs to the Cine Paris in Plaka's roof garden for an all-night blockbuster treat. They say that when the wind blows on screen at the Cine Paris, gusts fan the audience from across the Acropolis – right on cue. And if the movie stinks, simply turn your attention to the neighbouring apartments and open windows: a rich treasure-trove of soap opera storylines and comedy drama that airs night after night.

Magical Athenean views at twilight.

081

SKYROS

CONTACTS
Skyros Holidays
Tel: +44 (0)1983 865 566
Fax: +44 (0)1983 865 537
Email: office@skyros.com
www.skyros.com

Create solid foundations for your relationship through a shared yoga experience in the Greek sunshine.

Skyros Holidays has run its innovative breaks on this remote Greek island since the 1960s. Steeped in deep romantic nostalgia and age-old traditions, Skyros Island is a powerful setting that many claim offers up huge amounts of natural energy and positive thought. For this is the home of the Skyros Centre, nestled on the hillside at the edge of Skyros village, set high above narrow, cobblestoned streets and pleasant beaches. Shaded by fig and pomegranate trees, the Skyros Centre boasts panoramic views of the valley and the deep blue waters of the Aegean. In this delightful setting, amidst bougainvillea and trailing vines, the unalloyed timeless beauty of Greece remains wholly untroubled by time.

So far around 20,000 guests have revelled in the uplifting force of Skyros enjoying early morning yoga together, aromatherapy massages, Greek dancing, local wines, hearty communal lunches and workshops that explore the origins of love. Woven throughout every aspect of the Skyros Centre is a positive, empowering ethos, be it the delicious, fresh, health-boosting organic cuisine or the magical, mood-enhancing moonlit walks. Free of their daily routine, guests are encouraged to reassess their priorities. Sound a bit like hippy psychobabble? Don't knock it: the effect is quite extraordinary, even in a short weekend. Smiles are broader, people walk taller and furrowed brows disappear. Couples are more connected, hearts grow bigger and spirits are uplifted. For in this sun-drenched romantic setting, life seems to make more sense.

Many couples rarely find the time to explore the ideas and dreams that flow over a shared bottle of wine. Busy lives hold us back, our spirits need uplifting and we lack focus and direction. Dubbed 'sunshine for the soul', Skyros is a name that evokes an overwhelming sense of hope as a place where friendships are forged, connections are formed and relationships strengthened. 'Love made visible' forms the heart of every community on Skyros. Explore yoga, holistic health, spa pampering, art, music and the island's natural splendour in this romantic island retreat now immortalised in evocative plays, poetry and song.

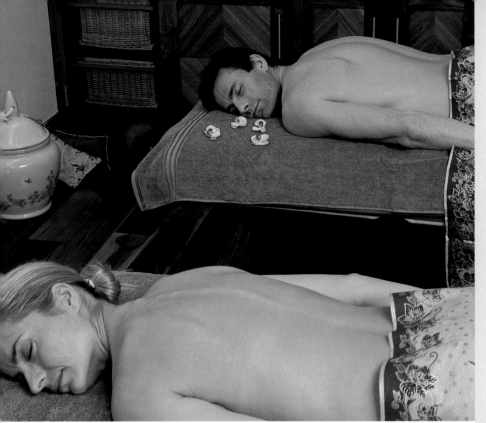

CONTACTS

Apsenti Boutique Resort
Tel: +30 228 90 24 015
Fax: +30 228 90 26 622
Email: info@apsenti.com
www.apsenti.gr

Mykonos Tourist Office
Tel: +30 228 90 23 990
Fax: +30 228 90 22 229

*Enjoy a relaxing massage for
two to soft music.*

MYKONOS

On the west side of the island of Mykonos a doorman shields his eyes from searing rays of the midday sun. "Welcome to the dream," he smiles, extending a welcome as warm as climate. Drenched in myths of love and lust, Mykonos is famous for its sensual interchange of colours – the deep blue of the Aegean edging golden rocks and highlighting flowers of white and pink. In this most seductive natural setting, the Apsenti offers romantic refuge: a boutique hotel exclusively for couples, encircled by flickering lanterns beneath a moonlit sky. Pampering and cosseting is a perfected art form here with considerable detail dedicated to romance, from candlelit dinners and massages for two to soft music and queen-size beds. Sumptuous blood-red sunsets arrive bang on cue to embrace the shoreline's rugged splendour, a romantic pre-dinner spectacle.

Accommodation at the Apsenti is individually styled with romantic couples in mind. Each room and suite is appropriately named to evoke the spirit of romantic endeavour, from the Love Nest and Sweet Hug to the Love Affair. Popular with honeymooners, both straight and gay, the Apsenti's decor is soothing, seductive and sumptuous. Gorgeous, flowing white curtains and pale-rose beading are adorned with entwined, trailing Greek vines and ribbons. Many rooms have private terraces with striking sea views and relaxation couches, others have sunken whirlpool baths and private flower-filled gardens, all offer total privacy and come with exotic fruit platters and a bottle of wine. Take a dip in the pool under a sparkling, star-filled sky, cuddle up in a hammock or enjoy a sensuous, honey-infused olive oil couples' massage. A romantic Mykonian ambience truly envelops Apsenti after dark when a zillion carefully positioned lamps begin to emit a subtle glow from limestone nooks and crannies, casting evocative shadows that dance to the gentle sounds of the sea. Enjoy fresh seafood and fine Champagne in an intimate dining setting of exposed stone. There is even a tiny white-stone chapel should you decide to pop the question amidst the hundreds of white candles and the sweet fragrance of the island's blooms.

*Raise a glass to romance
on the Island of Aphrodite.*

CYPRUS

In Denise Larkin's contemporary novel, an evocatively penned narrative explores the romance of Cyprus, Aphrodite's isle. The Island of Love is a tale of heartfelt passion, lust and stolen kisses that draws a compelling parallel between the Island's ancient myths and modern-day stories of love. As the inspiration of poets, philosophers and writers since ancient times, Cyprus' romantic, rugged, wave-hemmed shoreline provides a dramatic, storied backdrop to ardour, where soulful affection, tender moments, yearning and adoration are a common theme. At the heart of every Cypriot there lies a passion for family, love, food, wine, beauty and the island's classical mythology. Of the island's sea-born Goddess of Love, Aphrodite, Percy Bysshe Shelley famously wrote: *"the beautiful is born; sea and earth, may well revere the hour of that mysterious birth…"*.

Although legend states that Aphrodite emerged from the boulder-scattered waves in 1200 BC, the spirit of the Goddess remains evident to this day. Islanders point to a dove's lissom wings, the silky petals of a poppy and fragrant scent of a rose as sacred mementoes of Aphrodite. Yet she has greater metaphoric power than this, she represents Cyprus. Signs welcome visitors with: "Cyprus, Island of Aphrodite" while passengers travel Aphrodite Class on Cyprus Airways. A natural spring on the island's Akamas Peninsula is where Aphrodite quenched her thirst. Today, courting couples share a sip in a declaration of love, prompting Italian poet Arioste to write: *'take a sip from it and even today love may materialize'*. In art, the Goddess continues to represent fantasy and desire while island-wide, Cypriot's sip full-bodied Aphrodite wine.

Romantics keen to experience the Cypriot Island of Love's warm sentiment can raise a glass to Aphrodite in the charming village of Koilani between Ayios Amvrosios and Pera Pedi close to Limassol on the coast. For a pinprick-sized community, Koilani boasts an extraordinary history steeped in old wine-making traditions and Aphrodite myth. As the home of four vineyards, the tradition of winemaking is endemic to the region's centuries-old cultural identity, employing local villagers and maintaining an age-old craft. October's Grape Festival celebrates the end of the harvest with folk-dancing, music, food and of course, wine. Grand ceremonial gestures honour the Gods in ancient ceremonial rituals while toasts pay tribute to Aphrodite, Adonis and Eros amidst olive groves, old white-washed stone buildings and tumbling vines.

TURKEY

Turkey's rich history can be traced back to Neolithic times. Today, this southeast European nation occupies a smaller span of the northwest Middle East, bordered to the southeast by Georgia, Armenia, Iran, Iraq and Syria and to the west with Bulgaria and Greece. As an East-meets-West gateway, Turkey links the old worlds of Asia, Africa and Europe and has a hybrid culture derived from a hotchpotch of stimuli, especially in the ultra-cosmopolitan city of Istanbul. Turkey's rural areas remain deeply traditional and reliant on the landscape, from the soaring mountains that run parallel to the coast and broad plains and plateaux to the fishing settlements of the Black Sea region and large tracts of natural forest.

TIME DIFFERENCE GMT +2

TELEPHONE CODE +90

CURRENCY New Turkish Lira

LANGUAGE Turkish

POPULATION 71.1 million

SIZE OF COUNTRY 780,580 sq km (304,426 sq miles)

CAPITAL Istanbul

WHEN TO GO Because of Turkey's geographical location, pinpointing a single climate is tricky as the weather spans from moderate and temperate to long, hard winters. A Mediterranean climate in western Anatolia offers average temperatures of 9°C (48°F) in winter and 29°C (84°F) in summer, while the snowy plateau regions can reach winter averages of -2°C (28°F). On the Black Sea coast, a wet, warm and humid summer climate (23°C/73°F) and mild winters (7°C/45°F) forms a sharp contrast to eastern Anatolia where harsh winters see snow cover from November until the end of April and temperatures of around -13°C (9°F).

TOURIST INFORMATION
Turkish Culture & Tourism
Tel: 020 7839 7778
Fax: 020 7925 1388
Email: info@gototurkey.co.uk
www.gototurkey.co.uk

084

ISTANBUL

CONTACTS
Ritz Carlton Istanbul
Tel: +90 212 334 44 44
Fax: +90 212 334 44 55
www.ritzcarlton.com

Byzas Tours
Tel: +90 212 2257 670
Fax: +90 212 2257 669
Email: info@toursistanbul.com
www.byzastoursturkey.com

Turkey's exotic aura of romance has fascinated novelists of every genre, from Agatha Christie to Orhan Pamuk and Ottoman intrigue to Byzantine mystery. Richly interwoven scenic pleasures so beautifully evoke the complex Turkish myths, with snow-peaked mountains that rise up from rugged savannahs and legend-steeped ancient coastlines. The quintessentially Eastern city of Istanbul, at the crossroads of Europe and Asia, stirs up the romantic essence of Turkey with its dazzling mosques, towering spires and opulent palaces. Calls to the faithful mix with the city's urban musical cacophony of Persian folk classics, Janissary marches and Turkish DJ beats. Ancient riches glitter amidst the relics of crusaders and sultans on the enigmatic moonlit waters of the dreamy Istanbul Strait.

Istanbul's waterway, an oft-cruised stretch hemmed by gorgeous amber-coloured minarets and domes, denotes the East-meets-West border. Named from the Greek word *bosphoros*, meaning a river, ford, or ferry, this vast, sweeping, bridge-straddled expanse is characterized by steep, craggy banks. Assumed to be a direct geological formation from the breaching of the Black Sea by the Mediterranean, the Bosporus has been long-revered for its romantic conations and strategic might. Today the riverbanks are home to the most lavish hotels in

Istanbul, many of which are bathed in Ottoman-inspired splendour that pays homage to Turkey's rich historical traditions. Drawing on the aged principals of the city's architectural heritage, the Istanbul Ritz Carlton fuses rich contemporary style with elegant domes, columns, mosaics and vaulted ceilings so evocative of olden Istanbul.

Somehow romance seems effortless at the Ritz Carlton, where smiling, attentive staff are primed to deliver impeccable service in a hotel that prides itself on perfecting the tiny details that make every stay unique. Located on the second floor of the hotel's highest tower, the Ritz Carlton's most sumptuous suite offers unforgettable panoramic views of the Bosporus Strait from a tiled bathtub for two. On an expansive private terrace, twinkling lanterns heighten the romance of this exquisite accommodation, where accents from the imperial Ottoman era complement sumptuous drapes and hand-woven Turkish carpets. Sip perfumed tea looking at a hazy star-lit sky, listening to the honking horns of passing ferries and enjoying the pungent aroma of charcoal and spices. Gaze out on chartered boats and public ferries traversing the waters from Eminonu on the Istanbul peninsula. Departures run every 45 minutes – or on demand – with a two-hour sunset champagne cruise costing 900 lira per person.

Revel in exotic East-meets-West romance on Istanbul's atmospheric waterway.

CONTACTS
Yasemin Yachting
Tel: +90 252 358 7094
Fax: +90 252 358 7093
Email: info@yaseminyachting.com
www.yaseminyachting.com

Bathe in the warm azure waters of Bodrum's coast.

BODRUM

Few modes of sea-travel evoke such nostalgic romance as a traditional wooden gulet, Turkey's handcrafted sailing vessel. Built for seafaring adventure and shipboard comfort, a gulet is synonymous with the timeless beauty of the Turquoise Coast and its coves and open seas. By far the easiest option is to hire a crewed gulet for a voyage that is plotted, navigated and sailed on your behalf. With all the chores taken care of, from the cooking and fishing to the cleaning, the breathtaking seascape can be fully enjoyed without breaking into a sweat. Simply relax on the boat's sun deck, snorkel in a rock-hemmed bay or take a refreshing dip in the crystal-clear waters. Pop open a bottle of fine champagne as an ever-changing vista rolls by under a sun-soaked sky past rugged cliffs, caves and ancient ruins. Marvel at idyllic, penny-sized atolls, beach-fringed bays, flying fish, dolphins, breathtaking sunsets and balmy, star-filled nights. With your captain at your side, revel in the onboard camaraderie surrounded by some of the earliest remnants of civilization and the world's richest cultural treasures.

Bodrum, originally settled in 12th century BC as Halikarnassos, was once home to Herodotus, the so-called 'father of history'. As Turkey's most popular resort, today Bodrum combines 5,000 years of history with world-class coastal amenities and is the launch point for most slow-paced gulet forays into ancient waters. Acknowledged as one of Europe's finest cruising regions, Bodrum's abundant sunshine, crystal clear waters, good anchorages and unspoiled areas rich in natural beauty hold enormous romantic appeal. Stunning shoreline landscapes are lapped by sparkling waters edged with beaches, olive groves, rocky crags and pine woods. Contrary to popular myth, an extraordinary array of hues characterize the Turquoise Coast, from the dark indigo tones of daytime to evening's pink-coloured waters. Homer wrote of a 'wine red sea' and the myriad rose-tinted hues mirror his script.

To voyage through the region's rich and storied past, follow the romantic route taken by Marc Anthony and Cleopatra who hid amongst the languid bays of the Turquoise Coast on passion-filled lovers' trysts. On their marriage, Anthony bestowed the region to his bride as a gift. Today the waters retain a romantic charm as the place where Cleopatra bathed during her honeymoon: shimmering, as befitting a gift to an Egyptian queen, and flushed with love.

UNITED KINGDOM

TIME DIFFERENCE GMT

TELEPHONE CODE +44

CURRENCY Pound sterling

LANGUAGE English

POPULATION 60.6 million

SIZE OF COUNTRY 300,000 sq km
(117,000 sq miles)

CAPITAL London

WHEN TO GO Surrounding seas ensure the UK
has a year-round temperate maritime climate with
variable, unpredictable weather that can change
from day to day. Winters are cool, while summers
are warm, if wet. Temperatures rarely dip much
below 0°C (32°F) or reach higher than 29°C
(84°F), with stiff sea breezes around the coasts.

TOURIST INFORMATION
Visit Britain
Tel: 020 8846 9000
www.visitbritain.co.uk

For a small cluster of islands, the UK boasts a lot of contrasts,
with a wide variety of landscapes and diverse cultures whichever
direction you travel in. Made up of Great Britain (England, Scotland
and Wales) and Northern Ireland, the UK comprises numerous
distinct cultures, languages and traditions. Each unique country
retains its own architectural heritage and historical legacy. Ancient
cities and modern towns are surrounded by rural countryside rich in
agricultural communities, while bustling seaside resorts and coastal
villages maintain a seafaring tradition. Explore honey-stoned villages,
lakes, mountains, glorious national parks, beaches, plunging valleys
and even vineyards – and enjoy some of the world's most vibrant
and cosmopolitan cities.

BELFAST

Amidst the rolling, green wooded hills of Hollywood, the Culloden Estate's annual evening of opera provides a dramatic compliment to the stunning scenery that surrounds it. On a sunny weekend in mid-June, this fine historic hotel in Northern Ireland throws open its gardens to usher in free-flowing Champagne: a sophisticated, bubble-filled prelude to a grand operatic event. From great seducers, irresistible cads and romantic euphoria to gripping stories of passionate love, intrigue, adultery and death – Culloden's audience will experience them all, be it the lascivious Count in Mozart's Le nozze di Figaro or Britten's Death in Venice, based on Thomas Mann's symbolic story of a distinguished writer's fatal obsession. Jealousy and sexual fixation stir up powerful emotions in Bizet's Carmen while Verdi's masterpiece, Othello, turns Shakespeare's play about fatal passion into a *tour de force*.

The palatial Culloden Hotel luxuriates in a secluded 12-acre estate, part of a family-run enterprise, and is recognised as one of the Small Luxury Hotels of the World. It added opera to its long line of acclaimed endeavours in 2004 and now offers a full weekend programme; with Laurent Perrier as a sponsor, the event is a truly lavish affair. Weekending guests, together with around 500 of Belfast's finest, gather in the landscaped grounds overlooking Belfast Lough, each dressed to the nines. Ladies are presented with a single tall-stemmed white rose as they move from the garden into the auditorium where cabaret-style seating is arranged around tables of 10.

Despite the glitz, style and glamour, Culloden's opera is refreshingly free of ostentatious overkill, allowing the audience to engage with the performance without distraction. On an intimate scale, the drama unfolds on a small main stage but is interspersed with forays into the audience, providing a thrilling immediacy so often lacking in more traditional opera settings. To date, Co-Opera Ireland has presented each year's programme, most recently triumphing with a stunning performance of Pietro Mascagni's heart-rending *Cavalleria Rusticana* (Rustic Chivalry). Considered one of the classic verismo operas, *Cavelleria*

Rusticana caused a sensation when it premiered in Italy in the early 19th century, requiring Mascagni to take 40 curtain calls amidst a cascade of blooms. Co-opera Ireland has been similarly well-received, with rose-strewn Culloden rapturous with echoing applause well into the night after spellbinding renditions of *Rigoletto* and *Tosca*, led by charismatic maestro Michael Hunt.

CONTACTS
Culloden Estate & Spa
Tel: + 44 28 9042 1066
Fax: + 44 28 9042 6777
www.hastingshotels.com/Culloden

Imposing Culloden Castle – the ideal spot for a proposal?

CONTACTS
The Balmoral Hotel
Tel: +44 131 556 2414
Fax: +44 131 557 3747
Email: reservations.balmoral@
roccofortecollection.com
www.thebalmoralhotel.com

Edinburgh Tourist Board
Tel: +44 8452 255 121
Fax: +44 1506 832 222
Email: info@visitscotland.com
www.edinburgh.org

Scotrail
Tel: +44 845 601 5929
Email: scotrailcustomer.relations@
firstgroup.com
www.scotrail.co.uk

EDINBURGH

The Balmoral spoils couples with sumptuous bedrooms that are hard to leave.

Innumerable Scottish superstitions centre on ancient romantic myth and legend. Others stem from age-old Scottish rituals and old wives' tales. Plucking a lady's name from a hat to pin to your jacket was a courtship convention observed in the Middle Ages, signifying a lasting partnership that prompted the phrase 'wearing his heart on his sleeve'. That Mary Queen of Scots met Lord Darnley for the first time on St Valentine's Day, 1565, spawned other sentimental convictions, while many still swear by the old Celtic belief that a true love is revealed by roasting chestnuts over a fire to see if they crackle or pop. At the heart of Scottish romantic myth lies the capital, Edinburgh, a city where a handsome, flag-topped fortified castle stands proud above the historic streets. As an age-old centre of poets, kings and writers, this UNESCO City of Literature excels at romance, from its larger-than-life heroes and heroines, love stories and themes of honour, to sweetheart fairytales. Today, couples can float love poetry written on a paper lotus across a pond in the St Andrew Square's Poetry Garden or can hire a kilt-clad Celtic bard to make a public proclamation of their heartfelt devotion in Princes Street.

Under the gaze of Edinburgh Castle, the city's iconic Balmoral Hotel boasts a long romantic history as the setting for the city's most glamorous weddings since 1902. Arguably Edinburgh's most prestigious address, the century-old building stands sentinel at Number 1, Princes Street, an award-winning, early 19th-century design now beautifully remodelled. Home to the chandelier-decked Sir Walter Scott Suite, the most romantic ballroom in the city, the Balmoral is famed for its ornate cornicing, opulent grandeur and magnificent castle views. Under auspicious Michelin–starred executive chef Jeff Bland, a weekend 'Simply Romance' package boasts a menu of outstanding gastronomy. An award-winning sommelier guides couples through the extensive wine cellar, from ruby-red Beaujolais and pale-pink Rosé to the flirtatious bubbles of fine Champagne. An understated weekend of romantic excess where stylish divine decadence reigns supreme is the Balmoral's mantra: first breakfast in bed, then a sensual Ytsara bathing spa ritual, before a glass of something sparkly in a rose petal-strewn room. A hint of Scottish romance hides amongst the subtle checks and tartans in the earthy tones of the moors, mists and mountains. Only natural fabrics are used throughout, from linens and silks to wools and leather. Artwork has also been selected to reflect evocative Scottish scenes of shimmering lochs, stags, golden eagles and Scottish poets. Guests can even stay in the very suite where J.K. Rowling penned the closing chapters of the final Harry Potter novel – her scribbled glee on a stucco bust is on proud display.

With its majestic clock tower, revolving brass-trimmed doors and kilted footmen the Balmoral Hotel thrives on Edinburgh's hustle and bustle. While many can claim to have Edinburgh's landmarks on their doorstep, few can say their doorstep is the landmark itself. Nobody knows just how many photographs are taken of the sporran-clad doormen each year, but it easily runs to four-figures. As a home-from-home to many of the Scottish capital's most famous visitors, the Balmoral has 188 bedrooms, including 20 suites of which the magnificent Scone & Crombie Suite is the jewel in the crown. Original artworks, fine antiques and opulent fabrics sit amongst 1,500 square feet of spacious

elegance with Regency furniture, open fires, gilded mirrors and alabaster fireplaces.

As a recent addition to Condé Nast Traveller's Gold List (US edition) the Balmoral has received high praise for its newly revamped spa. A romantic theme prevails around the Roman bath-like, softly lit pool with its plasterwork columns and peaceful serenity. Snuggle up in a robe the size of a duvet and flop down on a day-bed to the gentle trickle of a water cascade. The introduction of a Bath Butler Service ensures spa-goers experience the epitome of luxurious service, namely a whole menu of speciality drinks, and treats such as chocolate-dipped strawberries delivered in person, at whim. Similarly, guests who prefer to remain romantically holed-up in their suite can call on the Butler for a range of Molton Brown aromatic oils and sensuous bath treatments. Designed to relax, pamper, indulge and seduce, Blissful Templetree offers an infusion of exotic plants and bioactive extracts from the Indian Ocean. Simply pour two glasses of champagne while your bath is run at the ideal temperature by the Bath Butler, then hop in with your partner – and enjoy.

The facilities at the Balmoral are second-to-none.

088

CORNWALL

CONTACTS

Tintagel Visitors Centre
Tel: +44 1840 779 084

Unique Homestays (Sea Nook)
Tel: +44 1637 881 942
Fax: +44 1637 882 019
www.uniquehomestays.com

Port William public house
Tel: +44 1840 770 230

Harbour Restaurant, Port Isaac
Tel: +44 1208 880 237

Rick Stein restaurants
www.rickstein.com

Ripley's, St Merryn
Tel: +44 1841 520 179

Fifteen Cornwall
Tel: +44 1637 861 000

The craggy coves and windswept beaches of Cornwall's coastline are the ideal spot for indoor and outdoor indulgence.

As the birthplace of the noble King Arthur, the rugged, wave-lashed north Cornish coastline boasts an 800-year history rich in medieval legends of awe-inspiring drama and doomed romance. Facing the full force of the Atlantic, the skeletal remains of medieval Tintagel Castle evoke the romantic era of the knights of King Arthur, as captured by Lord Tennyson in his Idylls of the King. After a period as a Roman settlement and military outpost, Tintagel is thought to have been a trading settlement of Celtic kings during the 5th and 6th centuries. Yet it is the remains of Tintagel's stout but crumbling 13th-century royal castle, clinging precariously to jagged cliffs, that truly catch the breath – a rain-battered and windswept memory of feasting Arthurian knights.

Built by Richard, Earl of Cornwall, younger brother of Henry III, the castle was used as a Cornish stronghold by subsequent Earls of Cornwall. Despite extensive excavations since the 1930s, Tintagel Castle remains one of Britain's most spectacular and romantic spots, evoking a glorious medieval era. Tales of Merlin's cave and spellbinding magic merely add to its enchantment and charm. Destined to remain a place of mystery and romance, Tintagel (from the Cornish *dyn tajel*, meaning 'narrow-necked fort') is steeped in tales of Camelot, Guinevere and the brethren of the Round Table. That this heavily fortified stronghold sits on one of Europe's most mysterious coastlines simply adds to its splendour.

An ancient medieval coastal trail stretches to Tintagel from one of North Cornwall's most scenic sandy beaches, Trebarwith Strand. Nestled in the bottom of a deep valley, and shrouded by a shield of rocks and boulders, the beach enjoys spectacular views out to sea and is only accessible at low tide. Craggy caverns hide amongst a spine of pale, rocky cliffs overlooking the mammoth mass of Gull Rock offshore. High on top of the peaks, a cosily converted fisherman's cottage offers stylish accommodation fused with traditional charm. Don your walking boots to discover the delights of the South West Coastal Path – right on your doorstep, a couple of miles inland from Trebarwith Strand – between

Port Isaac and Tintagel. Romantic Sea Nook is popular with lovers keen to stroll in tranquility through Trebarwith Strand's shallow surf. Sitting in 50 acres of farmland, Sea Nook boasts jaw-dropping vistas gloriously free of crowds. Newly renovated to offer a snug, contemporary cottage feel, the property is blessed with every mod con for the perfect romantic weekend by the sea. Luxurious details include an open-plan living area (complete with squishy sofas for snuggling up), en suite bathrooms and a country kitchen offering plenty of space and light. A wood-burning stove, TV, DVD player, Bose SoundDock digital music system, full Sky satellite package, wireless broadband connection and a selection of DVDs also feature. Sea Nook is an eco-friendly conversion with all water sourced from boreholes; the property is warmed by geothermal underfloor heating and guests are encouraged to separate recyclable rubbish.

An ideal retreat for beach lovers, walkers and foodie aficionados, Sea Nook is tucked away in a secluded, elevated position offering panoramic views from Tintagel across to Trevose Head. French doors lead onto the terrace and gardens from where you can take in the full glory of the stunning scenery. The cottage is also located right in the middle of north Cornwall's gastronomic heartland: the Port William pub, perched above the sand, is close at hand and the family-run Harbour Restaurant is located in nearby Port Isaac. A short drive further south to Padstow uncovers Rick Stein's cluster of acclaimed seafood eateries, Michelin-starred Ripley's at St Merryn and Jamie Oliver's Fifteen Cornwall, overlooking the golden sands at Watergate Bay.

Guests at Sea Nook are welcomed by a basket of Cornish goodies, including a bottle of wine, plus a hamper of organic groceries by request. Candlelit romantic meals for two can be organized courtesy of a private chef while you and your partner relax with a glass of local Camel Valley bubbly, a real success of Cornish viniculture. Alternatively, you could try a glass of fruit mead – the region's so-called honeymoon libation.

089

LONDON

CONTACTS

The Goring Hotel
Tel: +44 (0)20 7396 9000
Fax: +44 (0)20 7834 4393
www.goringhotel.co.uk

London Eye
Tel: +44 (0)870 990 8881
www.londoneye.com

Royal Parks
Tel: +44 (0)20 72982100
www.royalparks.org.uk

Enjoy a sumptuous suite at the Goring Hotel for a touch of urban decadence.

Idyllic, leafy royal parks, sunset river cruises and resplendent palaces ensure Londoners are spoilt for choice when it comes to a romantic treat. Umpteen jewels in the crown run from the city's gleaming horse-drawn carriages along the tree-lined avenues that lead to Buckingham Palace, to the velvety petals of the 30,000 roses of gardens in beautiful Regent's Park. London, a picturesque symbol of romance, provided the setting of a pivotal scene in David Lean's classic British melodrama, the heartrending *Brief Encounter* (1945). It also plays host to the world's most famous love story, *Romeo and Juliet*, under open summer skies – simply add a Harrods picnic hamper and blooms from royal florist Moyses Stevens for an unforgettable star-lit evening of romance.

Similarly memorable is the romantic setting of the fine old English hotel, The Goring. Run for almost a century by four generations of the same family, The Goring has long been a bastion of proudly upheld, age-old tradition and boasts a historic location behind Buckingham Palace. Garden space in London's busy centre is a scarcity so the lush flower-filled and topiary-hemmed setting at The Goring is a true urban oasis. Enjoy delicious cocktails inspired by old-fashioned English recipes on a charming terrace, where servants of the Royal Household are as likely to be enjoying the quiet birdsong as a starry-eyed couple chinking glasses in romantic celebration. Delight in a delicate elderflower Martini, a highball of vodka combined with blackberries and blueberries squeezed with fresh lemon, or a shot of Cox's apple juice laced with vodka, wild water mint, honey, fresh ginger and lime. Simply phone ahead to add a myriad of romantic touches to a rendezvous, perhaps heart-

A private pod under a starlit sky has become a classic London experience for romantics.

shaped canapés and a jug of passion-fruit cordial served under graceful bronze sculptures and sweet-smelling flowers.

After a decadent evening of romance, consider sharing a rowing boat on the Serpentine's glassy depths at Hyde Park, one of London's finest historic parks covering 142 hectares. Over 4,000 trees and numerous meadows surround one of the most famous waterscapes in England, so named because of its languid, snake-like curves. Wending from Kensington Gardens into Hyde Park, this spring-fed expanse is one of London's most pleasant with the Serpentine Lido a romantic spot in which to share a refreshing summer dip. Created in 1730 by damming the Westbourne River, a small tributary of the Thames, in order that Queen Caroline might have a spot at which to enjoy the royal yachts, people have been bathing in these regal waters for hundreds of years. Grab a deckchair, spread out a blanket and enjoy London's continental-style respite amongst quacking ducks and romantic picnickers.

In the late afternoon light, lose your head high above the city bustle – at 135 m (443 ft) above the city, the London Eye is the world's tallest cantilevered observation wheel, offering breathtaking views across the capital's historic skyline. Carrying 800 passengers per revolution (equivalent to 11 of London's famous red double-decker buses), the London Eye's 32 capsules each weigh 10 tonnes, the equivalent of over a million pound coins. Since the wheel first rotated in March 2000, the Eye has become an iconic landmark, a metaphoric symbol of modern Britain and the turning of a new century. Today it is a celebrated venue of hope and vision – and a popular setting for proclaiming love. Enjoy a glass of Laurent-Perrier champagne served in a romantic Cupid's Capsule; add Green & Black's sumptuous organic chocolates or pink champagne truffles from Charbonnel et Walker for an extra special touch, then cosy up to absorb views fit for a Queen – you can see all the way to Windsor Castle 40 km (25 miles) away on a bright, clear day. Come evening, share views of the Thames on the North bank between Hammersmith and Kew Bridge cuddled up in the bar at pocket-sized pub, The Dove over a glass of sparkling English apple cider. Every dark, wooden nook oozes London history in this off-the-beaten-track romantic gem; the best love seat in the house is up a cast-iron staircase perched on the roof. For unforgettable moonlight vistas take a boat along London's broad and famous waterway for a dinner cruise through sentimental aged towers, domes and spires. Captured in rapturous style by English poet William Wordsworth and immortalized by the brushstrokes of Turner and Reynolds, the Thames embodies the heart of London in geographic and spiritual terms.

LLANDUDNO

CONTACTS
Bodysgallen Hall & Spa
Tel: +44 (0)1492 584466
Fax: +44 (0)1492 582519
Email: info@bodysgallen.com
www.bodysgallen.com
Weekend breaks start at £175 per
person per night.

Quay Hotel
Tel: +44 (0)1492 564 100
Fax: +44 (0)1492 564 115
www.quayhotel.com

Conwy Castle
Tel: +44 (0)1492 592358
www.conwy.com

*Tea for two in Bodysgallen's
cosy, fire-warmed interiors.*

To stroll through the magnificent gardens of Bodysgallen Hall is to become lost in 200 acres of colour-filled parkland, along pebble-stone paths hemmed by sweet-scented herbs. Perched high on a hill above the Victorian coastal town of Llandudno, Bodysgallen is home to a rare 17th century parterre of flowerbeds, topiary, clipped box hedges and cutwork shrubs, similar in style to the Palace of Versailles. Striking use of textures such as low-lying camomile, sunken beds and grasses add an extra dimension. Other features include naturally occurring limestone outcrops, waterfalls, rockeries, sundials, a walled garden, lily ponds, a croquet lawn and several follies.

Various springs traverse the parklands together with a riddle of leafy woodland walks. Meander out to a crumbling Gothic Tower on the summit of Pydew Mountain through rose gardens, mulberry trees and mature shrub-covered areas, both manicured and wild. Believed to have 13th-century origins, Bodysgallen Hall's fine gardens enjoy magnificent views of Conwy Castle and the mountains of Snowdonia and are admirably maintained by gardener Robert Owen and his long-serving team. Grab a glass of vintage Champagne for a guided tour around the grounds in summer and early autumn.

Constructed in the Middle Ages as a defensive tower house for nearby Conwy Castle, Bodysgallen Hall hides away amongst dense woodland shielded from prying eyes. Today, only the chimney tops of this 'house among thistles' (as Bodysgallen is said to mean) are visible. Much of the original 13th-century structure is wholly intact and despite the gradual addition of one wing, then another, during a building history of 600 years, the whole house is built in the same sturdy, conservative style. Handsome heraldic arms and fine antiques are best enjoyed over Bodysgallen's traditional Welsh afternoon tea – plus a glass of the sparkly stuff.

Lady Augusta Mostyn restored any faddish blunders to the vernacular architecture of the house for her son and her sensitive hand remains evident throughout Bodysgallen today. Donated to the National Trust by businessman Richard Broyd in 1997, Bodysgallen remains committed to an ongoing programme of preservation – the award-winning gardens alone are acclaimed the world over. Climb the narrow, winding stone staircase for truly awesome views of the fortified towers of storied Conwy Castle, one of the great fortresses of medieval Europe with its eight mighty towers and high curtain walls that appear to rise up out of the hills. Romantic weekend breaks at Bodysgallen begin on arrival with a welcoming glass of chilled Laurent Perrier. Guests can also enjoy anti-stress hot stone massages in the spa, together with admittance to Conwy Castle. Stroll along the River Conwy's estuary path to the stylish waterfront Quay Hotel for a romantic cocktail in the upper-level bar to enjoy resplendent sunset views. Then return to Bodysgallen to dine in elegant historic surroundings. According to Men's Health magazine, Bodysgallen Hall 'will cause the most jaded of you (to) consider proposing marriage, if you haven't already'; it is just as well that the wine cellar is kept well stocked.

IRELAND

This lush, green, rugged island in the North Atlantic Ocean is separated from Britain by the choppy Irish Sea. Flat, low-lying plains are fringed by a ring of coastal mountains with Carrauntoohil the highest peak at 1,041 m (3,435 ft). Numerous rocky islets, peninsulas and outcrops hem Ireland's craggy shoreline, with the River Shannon at 259 km (161 miles) flowing south to north to meet the sea. Undulating hills offer some of the most varied and unspoilt scenery in Europe while 5,600 km (3,480 miles) of coastline offer plenty of quiet sandy beaches. The inspiration of centuries of poets, artists and writers, Ireland's volcanic lunar landscapes lie lapped by fertile pasture and flower-filled meadows. Northern Ireland, in the northeastern part of the island, is part of the United Kingdom.

TIME DIFFERENCE GMT

TELEPHONE CODE +353

CURRENCY Euro

LANGUAGE English and Irish Gaelic

POPULATION 4.1 million

SIZE OF COUNTRY 70,280 sq km (27,409 sq miles)

CAPITAL Dublin

WHEN TO GO Ireland's prevailing warm, moist Atlantic winds and temperate climate characterize a landscape lavished with rainfall. Mild winters lead to cool summers, with May to September the driest period. Short, wet, foggy days predominate from November to February.

TOURIST INFORMATION
Discover Ireland
Tel: +44 (0)20 7518 0800
Fax: +44 (0)20 7493 9065
www.discoverireland.com

DUBLIN

GETTING THERE
The airports at Kerry (45mins) and Cork (1hr 15mins) are both served by several daily flights from London and Dublin

CONTACTS
Sheen Falls Lodge
Tel: +353 644 16 00
Fax: +353 644 13 86
Email: info@sheenfallslodge.ie
www.sheenfallslodge.ie

Few romantic picnics are as memorable as a table for two by a tumbling waterfall, deep in dappled woodlands.

As the sun sets over the looming peaks of MacGuillicuddy Reeks and Kenmare Bay, the sound of the water takes on a mellow, rhythmical motion guaranteed to nurture restful sleep. As candles are lit one by one in the surrounding gardens, a resident pianist warms up the ivories on a baby grand piano. Outside, a gleaming 1990 Rolls Royce Silver Spirit 11 patiently awaits your arrival, a gourmet champagne supper hamper at the ready. Renowned for its stunningly lush, green scenery, Sheen Falls Lodge sits amidst the hidden countryside of Ireland's southwest. Centuries of true explorers have marvelled at this barren, rugged landscape where windswept beauty and a foreboding sense of excitement intertwine. On a raw, untamed coastline, a puzzle of leafy walking trails boast extraordinary views across a shoreline steeped in romance under the jagged crags of Ireland's highest mountains, set against a misty sky. The landscape of Kenmare Bay provides an ever-changing backdrop, unveiling a myriad of tidal hues beyond woodlands where wild deer and other fauna roam free.

As a privately owned country house hotel, Sheen Falls Lodge boasts easy access to three of Ireland's airports, Shannon, Cork and Kerry. Just off the famously scenic Ring of Kerry, a 10-minute drive from the brightly coloured village of Kenmare,

the Lodge is only 30 minutes away, in the heathery countryside of Killarney. Much of the original building dates back to the 1600s; the first stones were laid with no knowledge that it would someday become one of Ireland's most magnificent 5-star romantic retreats. As the summer residence of the Marquis of Lansdowne, the house once welcomed the salmon-fishing and deer-hunting gentry. Today, it greets couples from all over the world as a haven of peace, good taste and tranquillity.

Three acclaimed restaurants range from classic elegance to bistro and lounge dining where good Irish produce and local recipes take pride of place. Contemporary cocktails, Irish malts and local ales are served in the relaxed, club-like atmosphere of the cosy bar with its dark wood and leather chairs. The estate, cradled between the Caha Mountains and the Kenmare Bay, hosts a multitude of historic tales such as the ruins of a tiny Viking-era church and a holy well reputed to have healing waters. Journey – in the Lodge's chauffeured Rolls Royce – out to pretty coastal villages blessed by innumerable native plant species that thrive in the Gulf Stream-warmed climate, or simply enjoy the quietude of nature on a foray along riverside pathways to discover the romantic secrets of lovers from years gone by.

GETTING THERE
The stables are a short drive from Dingle town and one hour from Kerry airport

CONTACTS
Dingle Tourism
Tel: +353 669 15 11 88
Email: info@dingle-peninsula.ie
www.dingle-peninsula.ie

Dingle Horse-riding Holidays
Tel: +353 669 15 21 99
Email: info@dinglehorseriding.com
www.dinglehorseriding.com

A shared pony trek provides the perfect vantage point from which to explore the beautiful Dingle Peninsula together.

DINGLE

David Lean's beautifully shot film, *Ryan's Daughter* captured the rambling, romantic charm of the Dingle Peninsula, from the rugged earthiness of the landscape's rich, peaty soils to the lush, green mountains that characterize the Celtic terrain. Soaring peaks and a ribbon of country roads lined with golden gorse and flowering fuchsia present a dramatic checkerboard of textures above crashing Atlantic waves and ragged, rocky isles. Rolling pea-green meadows and mysterious forests lead to sandy beaches riddled with footpaths and bridle trails allowing scenic walks or leafy forays on the back of an Irish steed.

Couples keen to explore Dingle's raw natural beauty in the saddle will enjoy the proud, dependable companionship of an Irish horse, be it a tall, placid Irish Draught, an elegant piebald or a surefooted Irish Cob. Ireland's age-old equine tradition has earned it the name, 'Land of the Horse' and while Dingle is best suited to riders with some experience, confidence counts and a number of tour operators run leisurely half and full-day treks. Dingle's undulating countryside is

scattered with fossil-ridden relics, ancient stones and ruins that evoke the mysteries of civilisations past. Meander through heather-cloaked meadows to bird-scattered marshes and rich green pastures before picking your way down stone-scattered mountain slopes steeped in mythological legend. Pounding waves and screeching gulls sing rhythmic songs of the broken hearted while fields flecked with yellow blooms inspire poems in honour of souls lost.

Irish legend has it that friendships blossom and love grows in the saddle – a place where language, age and culture form no barrier to shared physical pursuit. Enjoy a gentle trot out to a half-timbered Irish inn for a glass of stout or a pot of tea by the fire, before exploring the bird-filled trails around Horseshoe Lake in the foothills of the chiselled Coomacarrea Mountains. Etched Petroglyphs inscribe the sculpted peaks of these eerie crags to mirror the knotty scrawls of the map's onward route. Amble along to the upper slopes in order to scour the water for a glimpse of Dingle's resident dolphins frolicking in the spray.

ICELAND

TIME DIFFERENCE GMT

TELEPHONE CODE +354

CURRENCY Iceland Krona

LANGUAGE Icelandic

POPULATION 299,000

SIZE OF COUNTRY 103,000 sq km
(40,170 sq miles)

CAPITAL Reykjavik

WHEN TO GO Iceland enjoys a cool temperate
ocean climate, thanks to the Gulf Stream, with
average July temperatures around 12°C (54°F)
and fairly mild winter conditions. Snow becomes
rain in spring, but is rarely more than a shower.
Peak season is the bright, crisp months of
May and June.

TOURIST INFORMATION
Icelandic Tourist Board
Tel: +354 535 5500
Fax: +354 535 5501
Email: info@icetourist.is
www.icetourist.is

Iceland's mystical landscape boasts some of Mother Nature's greatest triumphs, from tremendous icecaps, mammoth glaciers and spouting geysers to steaming solfataras, volcanoes and cascading waterfalls. Home to numerous birds and a prime location for whale-watching, Iceland's mild summers and snow-shrouded winters are ideal for the adventurous visitor. Explore the plains on horseback or take a dip in a gin-clear, glacial pool. All-consuming sunsets see the sky morph from egg yolk gold to an oily, inky-blue splashed with purple and crimson. Experience the exhilaration of 24-hour daylight from mid-June to mid-July each year during northern Iceland's celestial White Nights.

REYKJAVIK

Iceland's magical landscapes and fascinating cultures sit on one of Europe's last great natural wildernesses where striking unworldly terrain and glacial splendour combine. On a backdrop of mist-shrouded glacial waters and brooding ancient lava beds Iceland's jaw-droppingly rugged terrain is easily discovered just a 40-minute drive from the hubbub of the capital city. Cavernous gullies filled with gin-clear water from the melted frozen icecaps of the Hofsjokull Mountains sparkle in bright, white sunshine. Filtered by porous volcanic rocks, the clarity is astounding, with droplets hanging in their purest form like cut-glass chandeliers. A surreal, ethereal and dizzying experience, Iceland's Moon-like landscape encapsulates rolling meadow and ice-strewn tundra. Deep ponds, lava crags, canyons and sharp ravines hide amongst twisted volcanic spurts, scrub and vast lagoons.

Anyone who values authenticity in their wellness retreats will revel in Iceland's uniqueness. Restoration is achieved using pure, organic products in a natural setting where the focus is a symbiotic balance of three core elements: water, fire and earth. As one of the most geologically active places on the planet, Iceland is rich in geothermal energy and is the most isolated and least densely populated country in the western world. Spas harness Mother Nature in their therapies, from bubbling hot springs, mud pots, glaciers, geysers, volcanoes and lava deserts to its numerous lakes, rivers and waterfalls. Traditional health philosophies have long centred on the positive, curative effects of hot water and cold air on the human body, mind and soul. Take a dip in steam-hazed outdoor pools kept to a temperature of 29°C (84°F) before braving the heat of steam rooms and saunas. At 42°C (108°F), the Icelandic hot pot isn't for the faint-hearted – especially when followed by a heart-stopping plunge into an icy pool.

Iceland's famous Blue Lagoon boasts a plethora of unique mineral, silica and algae active properties used in therapies proven to have anti-aging benefits. Located just a 20 minute drive from Keflavík International Airport, the Blue Lagoon sits on around six-million litres of geothermal seawater that gurgles up in warm, brackish spouts at around 37–39°C (99–102°F). Naturally renewed every 40 hours, the water in this unique ecosystem is 100 per cent pure and chemical free. Relaxing treatments take place both inside and in the lagoon itself, from deep flotation (equivalent to eight hours of sleep) and gently rejuvenating lava-dust and clay massages, to nourishing shared circulation-boosters in seawater hot tubs for two.

CONTACTS
Iceland Retreats
Tel: +44 (0)7985 249 398
Email: info@icelandretreats.com
www.icelandretreats.com

Rain or shine, the Blue Lagoon is a unique experience – and one that is best shared.

GETTING THERE

Lake Myvatn is located in the remote north-east of Iceland, 100 km (62 miles) east of Akureyri on Route 1. In season (May–Aug), you can reach Lake Myvatn, by daily buses from Akureyri, Húsavík and Egilsstaóir. From early July to late August, there are buses from Reykjavik via the remote Sprengisandur route, with a change at Landmannalaugar. Between September and April four buses a week call at Myvatn.

CONTACTS

Lake Myvatn Hotel
Tel: +354 464 41 64
www.myvatn.is

The Aurora Borealis, viewed here from Lake Myvatn, are a breathtakingly romantic sight.

LAKE MYVATN

Bubbling mud flats and lunar-like volcanic craters characterize the striking terrain of Lake Myvatn, one of Iceland's most geologically active and stunningly beautiful regions. Renowned for its health-giving properties and spiritual energies, the lake and its 50 islands were declared a national conservation area in 1974 and boast extraordinary ancient lava spurts and mystical conical pillars from eruptions over many thousands of years. Steaming mud pools form boiling cauldrons across this austere, pock-marked terrain surrounded by looming mountains and glassy frozen lakes shrouded in a misty sulphuric haze.

Lake Myvatn's curative springs not only help skin gleam with vitality but are also said to calm, detoxify and de-stress. Yet what is most remarkable is the setting, an area of fragile beauty and enigmatic power, created by a vast fissure and a glowing molten flow of basaltic lava from the Laxardalur Valley. Today, Lake Myvatn's jagged landscape is dominated by explosions of rock in a volcanic forest of Ice Age post-glacial magma ridges and crags. Lying back in water-filled caverns to gaze up at a magical sky amidst a barren tree-less moonscape of hissing steam and carbon-coloured peaks is the romance of Mother Nature personified.

Every hotel in the Lake Myvatn region offers maps and tours out to the nature baths, simply pack a towel and follow the short walk to the healing waters of these warm, brackish pools. As shared romantic experiences outdoors go, few can compare with a dip in Lake Myvatn's natural baths where rustic geothermal pools offer couples steamy seclusion – often in a blizzard of giant snowflakes. Not that sub-zero temperatures form any barrier to the Icelandic tradition of enjoying nature to the full – oh no. Slipping blissfully into crystal-clear, warm therapeutic waters is a year-round past-time and feeling the heat seep deep into your bones in the depth of winter is very much the norm. You'll feel the positive effects of the mineral-rich waters after just 30 minutes as the vapour-laden bubbling *solfatars* work their magic – your skin will be soothed and softened and all will feel well with the world.

NORWAY

Norway's adoration of nature has made unspoiled green space a highly-prized national symbol. The virtues of parks, gardens, fjords and mountain trails are upheld with almost-religious zeal. Getting out into the fresh air is as much a part of the country's national identity as smoked salmon and peace-brokering. Over half of the Norwegian population have ready access to a cabin in the mountains while island cruises and country walks are popular romantic pursuits. Even in Oslo, city-dwellers have access to over 2,000 km (1,240 miles) of ski trails in surrounding forests, together with sculpture-scattered picnic spots.

TIME DIFFERENCE GMT +1

TELEPHONE CODE +47

CURRENCY Norwegian Krone

LANGUAGE Norwegian

POPULATION 4.52 million

SIZE OF COUNTRY 385,155 sq km (150,210 sq miles)

CAPITAL Oslo

WHEN TO GO Despite an extreme northerly position, Norway's mainland climate is surprisingly mild. The four seasons offer a considerable diversity of climate, with hot summer days and mountain skiing possible in the same 24 hours. Winters are cold but lose their bite in late April, when the parks, cafes and beaches spring back to life.

TOURIST INFORMATION
Visit Norway
Tel: 020 7389 8800
Fax: 020 7839 6014
Email: infouk@invanor.no
www.visitnorway.com

095

CONTACTS

Vigeland Park
Tel: +47 23 49 37 00
Fax: +47 23 49 37 01
www.vigeland.museum.no

Taste of Norway
Tordenskiolds 7, Oslo
Tel: +47 22 42 34 57

OSLO

In Norway, a picnic constitutes a bone fide meal, not a hurriedly grabbed, unimaginative snack. A mammoth array of delicacies is gathered for an al fresco Norwegian spread, from huge slabs of Jarlsberg cheese to plump strawberries, blueberries and cranberries. Piles of *wienerbrød* (a sweet pastry), *kaffebrød* (coffee bread), cookies, apple cake, waffles and cinnamon biscuits sit amongst crusty loaves and dimpled crackers. Then there is Norway's unique sticky-sweet *geitost* – caramelized goats' milk lactose without which no picnic is deemed complete.

Unlike many capital cities, Oslo's picnickers have the rural bread basket of the nation to hand at delicatessen Taste of Norway, where the motto, 'Quality, Not Quantity' is displayed with pride. Everything imaginable for the perfect outdoor meal is stocked in this gastronomic institution, from glazed meats and chalk-white cheeses to jars of homemade jams and jellies; eggs in brine, cured sausages, crabmeat, prawns, smoked fish pate and sliced venison all vie for attention. Then, of course, there is the finest smoked salmon in the world, sold whole or in slices or chunks. For a romantic picnic for two, let the staff at the shop know what you are planning; if you're intending to eat your gourmet haul immediately, they'll often throw in serviettes, straws and taster samples as part of the deal.

Hop aboard bus 20 or tram 12 out to the city's western suburbs to Vigelandsparken (Vigeland Sculpture Park), Oslo's premier picnic spot and a favourite with handholding romantics. Created by Gustav Vigeland, this breathtaking outdoor art gallery combines vast expanses of green open space with some of the finest bronze and granite sculptures in the world. One stunning masterpiece after another presents itself in a dazzling array during a lazy stroll through Vigeland's 80 acres, a total of 212 that form six themes, all related to human emotions, love and life. Set around pathways, trees, hedgerows and ponds of duck and geese, Vigeland's Monolith Plateau consists of 121 figurines protruding upwards in a knotted tower while his touching works depict tender young love. Witness entwined bodies and affectionate shared kisses in a panorama that captures the hearts and minds of visiting lovers amidst the embrace of sweeping, grassy slopes and gently swaying trees.

Witness powerful figurative sculptures – dedicated to life and love – under a dense blue sky at Oslo's Vigelandsparken.

CONTACTS
Destination Hardanger Fjord
Tel: 5655 3870
www.hardangerfjord.com

White Lady Fjord Cruises
Tel. +47 55 25 90 00 / 94 56 67 32
Fax. +47 55 25 90 01
www.whitelady.no
Cruises operate from May to
end of September.

*Take a little time out for
romance with Norway's
spectacular fjords as
a dramatic backdrop.*

BERGEN

Umpteen romantic tales owe much to Norway's luminescent, cliff-hemmed fjords and Norse mythology and it is easy to see why. Deep-blue, sparkling waters run like a silk scarf through a rugged, white-rocked terrain while an unworldly bright light reflects these incredible hues beacon-like up to the heavens. Mysterious crags dotted with vibrant flowering scrub hide amongst the fjords' dramatic peaks while jutting rock ledges provide the most spectacular coastal views. One such jaw-dropping panorama is found in Hardangerfjord in the west of Norway where a snow-topped glacial terrain and blossoming fruit trees evoke fairytale enchantment. Stretching for 179km between two ragged, milk-coloured spines, Hardangerfjord's rippling ribbon of tranquil sapphire moves effortlessly along to claim its place as the third largest fjord in the world.

Lined by numerous brick red-painted wooden villages, the Hardangerfjord lies 75 km (47 miles) east of Bergen amidst apple and cherry orchards riddled with hiking trails, waterfalls and mountain plateaus. From the mighty Atlantic Ocean, the Hardangerfjord winds northeasterly until it penetrates the imposing peaks of the Hardangervidda, reaching depths of 800 m (2,624 ft). Created by ancient flooded valleys and ice-melted torrents, the Hardangerfjord predates the Viking era and is steeped in Nordic legend as a once-remote and mythical land. Today as Norway's fruit basket, the region's rolling orchards are nourished by abundant natural gushing cascades – a truly breathtaking sight.

A number of meandering cruisers snake along the west coast of Norway to soak up the resplendent scenery around the shores of Bergen. The 27 m (89 ft), 100 passenger *White Lady* may be 65 years old, but her beautiful sculpted bow remains as graceful as ever. A large seated deck carries up to 100 passengers and contains several 'courting seats' for couples to share during daily departures. Expect to pay around 430 NOK for a four hour voyage of elegant refinement on one of Norway's most romantic waterways against a backdrop of sweeping, steep-sided inlets and bloom-studded ravines. Once back on land, raise a glass to the *White Lady* with a cocktail that shares her name at Bergen's UNESCO-protected, Hanseatic-era merchant quarter, the charming Hanseatic Wharf.

SWEDEN

TIME DIFFERENCE GMT+1

TELEPHONE CODE +46

CURRENCY Swedish Krona

LANGUAGE Swedish

POPULATION 9 million

SIZE OF COUNTRY 449,964 sq km
(175,486 sq miles)

CAPITAL Stockholm

WHEN TO GO Considering its northerly
geographic location (at the same latitude as parts
of Greenland and Siberia), Sweden enjoys a
favourable climate with mild, changeable weather
influenced by continental high pressure from the
east. Sunshine brings hot days in summer and
brightens cold winters. White nights (24 hour
sunlight) characterize land within the Arctic
Circle from late May until mid-July. Winter,
however, sees daylight diminish to around
5.5 hours a day in northern areas.

TOURIST INFORMATION
VisitSweden
Tel: +44 20 7108 6168
Email: uk@visitsweden.com
www.visitsweden.com

Sweden draws plenty of cultural sway from neighbouring Denmark
and Lapland in the Arctic north, adding simple country pleasures into
a swish urban mix. Sleekly modern cities ooze with sophistication,
yet Sweden's heart is in the unfussy romance of the mountains,
beaches and off-shore isles. As the fifth largest country in Europe,
Sweden is largely concentrated in the urban areas of Gothenburg
and Stockholm. Vast swathes of pine forest, fishing lakes and
mountains remain wholly undisturbed: an unworldly vision during
summer's Midnight Sun and the dizzying lights of the Aurora Borealis.

GOTHENBURG

For centuries, the Scandinavian concept of true relaxation has centred on three core principals. First, achieving an almost spiritual connection with nature; second, enjoying delicious fresh food and good company, thirdly, using fire, ice and water to heat and cool the body in rapid succession to physically rejuvenate and banish all ills. At the pine-shrouded Thorskogs Slott Castle, just a 30-minute drive north of Gothenburg, all three notions combine. In the grandest leafy parkland setting, amidst wood-fired hot tubs and steamily sensuous saunas, you'll find a sumptuous menu of award-winning Swedish cuisine. Tranquility abounds in this elegant resting place where 'lazy romantic weekends' are a speciality – Scandinavian style, of course. On the principal that time is the most precious gift we ever offer each other, Thorskogs Castle helps couples redress the balance, amidst fairytale turrets and duck-filled ponds

Thorskogs' magic starts working over a long, leisurely breakfast accompanied by birdsong and pots of home-roasted, freshly ground coffee. A soothing mellowness engulfs the castle as sunlight dances delicately across tufted spruce forests woven by dozens of leaf-shrouded paths. Outsized rooms characterize the castle's plush interior with sweeping drapes, a grand piano, chandeliers, antiques and fine art. The restaurant is celebrated throughout West Sweden and offers a menu of innovative Scandinavian dishes including a rather spectacular halibut terrine. The chef smokes the salmon himself over alder wood while the castle's eggnog is deserving of raptures – and a second helping.

On the banks of the scenic River Göta Älv, the original 13th-century manor house was frequented by royalty, nobility, courtiers, and aristocrats but was replaced in 1892 by Thorskogs Castle. Bought by current owners, Lena and Tommy Jonsson in 1986, it has been lovingly transformed to offer five star sanctuary for stressed urban couples keen to enjoy the good life without the pressures of a ticking clock. Thorskogs' romantic weekend packages are hugely popular and include luxurious robes, exotic fruit platters, a sauna and sparkling wine. To share a traditional fire-heated wooden bath tub under the stars amidst the pines, be sure to book prior to arrival; it is hard to imagine bathing in a more sublime setting – no wonder the Swedes are so relaxed.

CONTACTS
Thorskogs Slott
Tel: +46 520 66 10 00
Fax: +46 520 66 09 18
Email: info@thorskogsslott.se
www.thorskogsslott.se

Gothenburg Tourist Office
Tel: +46 31 61 25 00
Fax: +46 31 36 84 21 8
Email: turistinfo@goteborg.com
www.goteborg.com

Enjoy the health benefits of a rejuvenating sauna.

KIRUNA

CONTACTS
Ice Hotel
Tel: +46 980 668 00
Fax: +46 980 668 90
Email: info@icehotel.com
www.icehotel.com

Lapland is the quintessential winter wonderland, a romantic, frosty landscape of snow-covered pine trees, frozen rivers and deep snow. In this ice-crystal setting, there is something vaguely romantic about being dressed in long-johns and stuffed into a sleeping bag – even when you are awarded a certificate to congratulate you on surviving a sub-zero night.

Without daylight, Sweden's Ice Hotel basks in the mysterious 24-hour glow of polar skies. Yet step inside the reindeer-skin covered doors and the interior takes your breath away. Beautifully crafted ice pillars and ice-hewn furniture are cleverly woven with fibre optic lighting to ensure a mellow flicker in this glistening palace where temperatures shiver as low as -35°C (-31°F). Constructed from scratch each November, the Ice Hotel is built using ice blocks from the frozen Torne River. Come May, or earlier if there is a heatwave, the walls begin to melt. Located 160 km (100 miles) above the Arctic Circle, the snow is easily skiable in winter, with sleighs and dog-sleds for romantic exploration into Lapland's wilds. You may even get an audience with the ethereal Northern lights.

Each of the hotel's bedrooms is close to the Absolute Ice Bar, which is just as well as the pre-bed ritual involves several stiff, warming drinks. Clothing removal – how, where and when – can easily become an obsession in plummeting temperatures, however serene the aura. Beds are shrouded in thermal sleeping bags and heavy reindeer-skin rugs and aid a cosy, deep and restful sleep. Few early morning rituals are more romantic than defrosting together in the sauna – all part of the fun. The Ice Hotel concept was born in the 1990s when the people of Jukkasjärvi decided to turn minus temperatures into a plus. Inspired by visiting Japanese ice sculptors, French artist Jannot Derid exhibited his works in a specially constructed igloo built in the middle of the frozen River Torne. People journeyed long distances to witness the folly, including a couple from overseas that decided to stay overnight enveloped in reindeer furs. Today, over 15,000 couples have cuddled up in the world's first all-ice hotel. There is even an ice chapel in which vows can be exchanged in ice-encrusted splendour – with ice-hewn glasses for the toast.

A stay at the Ice Hotel – complete with dog-sledding – is the ultimate in snuggled-up romance.

CONTACTS
Stockholm Visitors Board
Tel: +46 850 82 85 00
Fax +46 850 82 85 10
Email: info@svb.stockholm.se
www.stockholmtown.com

*Stroll the harbourside together
in the land of the midnight sun.*

STOCKHOLM

Slick, sleek Stockholm boasts innumerable surprises. Just when you think you have the measure of Sweden's capital, something new comes out the blue – usually from the sky. With their pure, luminescent clarity, Stockholm's extraordinary skies have captured the hearts and minds of artists, poets and adventurers for centuries. In summer, Stockholm experiences the White Night phenomenon, when the sun waits until after midnight to dip below the horizon after hours of slowly unfolding, crimson-pink hues. Over the Midsummer holiday, extended daylight hours draw people out on the streets as the soft, warm glow of the so-called Midnight Sun bathes the city. Bars and restaurants rarely close in these barely dusk-like summer months. Pull up two chairs in a roof terrace cafe overlooking Sergels Torg to share a cafe latte at midnight and enjoy the unworldly romantic illumination of not the moon and stars, but the sun. What could be more romantic than a walk along the harbour at 3am in almost broad daylight, or to stroll hand-and-hand through Kungsträdgården in mood-enhancing radiance.

Head to the district of Södermalm to delve into an empty side-street where a steep set of stairs leads to the view-blessed Mosebacke restaurant. Resting on a hill in the heights of Södermalm and offering a panoramic vista over the city, Mosebacke's patio is easily one of the best places in Stockholm to sit with a loved one and watch the sun set during a summer evening, especially when the Aurora Borealis comes to play. Though it is rare for the Arctic Circle's jaw-dropping light phenomenon to cast its illuminating spell on Stockholm, it certainly does happen. In 2000, the city's skyline was silhouetted against an evocative emerald-green, neon inferno, a moving auroral display created by oxygen hovering over 240 km (150 miles) above the earth. When exposed to fast-moving particles from the magnetosphere, the light glows a blood-red crimson. Closer to home, it radiates as yellow-green – the most common auroral hue. In shared stupefaction, revel in the thrill of Mother Nature's vivid display of polar forces, the inspiration behind great lyricism and artistry at Sweden's celestial heart.

FINLAND

TIME DIFFERENCE GMT +2

TELEPHONE CODE +358

CURRENCY Euro

LANGUAGE Finnish

POPULATION 5.3 million

SIZE OF COUNTRY 337,030 sq km
(131,442 sq miles)

CAPITAL Helsinki

WHEN TO GO Bright spring March–April months
lead to magical summers of long, light-filled days
as city-dwellers exodus to the country en masse.
September–November is when Finland starts to
prepare for winter, while December–February
is snowy and icy although rarely without
some sunshine.

TOURIST INFORMATION
Visit Finland
www.visitfinland.com

Finish Embassy of London
Tel: 020 7838 6200
www.finemb.org.uk

As a nation, Finland is almost entirely shaped by its climate, exploding in a riot of colourful flowers and festivals in summer and revelling in winter snow and ice. Renowned for a down-to-earth natural purity in both its scenic splendour and human character, Finland is more than three-quarters covered in mysterious, dense coniferous forest. Cosy up in an igloo, fish amongst the ice, take a husky sled across the plains or watch the stars from a wood-fired sauna. Helsinki, the nation's buzzing capital, boasts historic Swedish-Russian influences, located on a peninsula reaching into the Baltic Sea.

CONTACTS
Igloo Village Kakslauttanen
Tel: +358 16 667 100
Email: hotel@ kakslauttanen.fi
www.kakslauttanen.fi

Snuggle up in your very own igloo, under a polar sky.

LAPLAND

In Scandinavian fairytale *Sneedronningen*, the Snow Queen revels in a magical land of frosted gardens dusted with crystallized, glittering ice. Shrouded in shimmering drapes, she holds court in a flurry of snowflakes (or 'snow bees') in an ice-frosted palace of snow-encrusted carpets and diamond-like sparkle and glitz. In real life, Mother Nature's bejewelled wintery lands offer an equal measure of snow splendour, a magnificent icescape of dramatic rolling snow hills and frosted gullies. Couples seeking an excuse to snuggle up close can do so in an ice-hewn igloo, wrapped in a feather-filled duvet with a hot chocolate night-cap, illuminated by the stars. These traditional arctic snow shelters have housed travellers for hundreds of years, and now benefit from some luxurious touches thanks to northern Finland's igloo-chic.

This most romantic Arctic foray is best enjoyed at the Igloo Village Kakslauttanen in Saariselkä where guests have their pick of 20 traditional dome-shaped igloos, including a honeymoon suite with uninterrupted views of the star-studded sky above. In warmer months (comparatively speaking), 37 rustic wooden cabins provide the accommodation each with a private sauna. Served by Ivalo airport, the resort opens each year

on the 1st December when temperatures settle between 0 and -5°C (32–23°F). Days are short from December to January, averaging five hours, but they benefit from a sublime, snow-reflective glow known as polar light. Given its extreme-north location, thick, fluffy snow is practically guaranteed in Kakslauttanen, where ultra-plump polar sleeping bags (designed for harsh, sub-zero conditions) ensure that a warm cosiness prevails.

Enjoy a heavenly cocktail in a stunning ice bar where 'chilling out' is taken to a whole new level, or dip into a piping hot sauna surrounded by frost-cloaked forests, before taking a courageous dip in gin-clear icy pools. Other arctic activities include romantic husky-drawn sledge rides and spectacular artwork of ice and snow, illuminated by the moon. Ice-lovers keen to begin married life in unique Arctic splendour can do so in an ice-encrusted chapel hung with reindeer skins. Forget fireworks, the Igloo Village has its own unforgettable wedding day finale, a jaw-dropping natural phenomenon best viewed in the Temple of Aurora Borealis. No laser show, neon light or firework display can compare with the atmospheric dazzle of the magnificent Northern Lights.

PAIJANNE

CONTACTS
Paijanne Tourism
Tel: +358 14 263 447 / 618 885
Fax: +358 14 665 560
Email: eija.hilden@prh.inet.fi
www.paijanne-risteilythilden.fi

Sweep a loved-one away to a wood cabin by tranquil Lake Paijanne – the most serene of romantic destinations.

In Russia a celebration calls for vodka, in Turkey raki, while in Cyprus it's a brandy sour. A glass of cava is raised in Spain while a whisky works its magic in Scotland. In Finland, weddings and special occasions are toasted with the ancient juniper-spiced local ale, sahti. Amidst vast taiga forests and bubbling volcanic springs, the Finns raise a glass of their cherished nectar to the Land of the Midnight Sun surrounded by wildflower-scattered summer meadows. Then it is time to feast on smoked meat, hoist the national flag and dance the polka, waltz and minuet with much laughter until dawn.

As one of the oldest, continuously brewed beers in the world, sahti's origins are shrouded in legend; it is thought to have played a role in the ancient pagan rituals of Finland's ancient Asiatic Ugrian forefathers from east of the Ural Mountains. Today it is much more than an ordinary Finnish beer (olut) and symbolizes joy, passion, friendship and merriment, and is an embodiment of the romantic country life. Best enjoyed with close companions, sahti is the shared toast of Finnish friendships and the celebration of betrothals, births and wedded unions, consumed in scenic lakeside settings and wooden cabins countrywide. Clink glasses with a loved one in a smoky, wood-fired sauna or whilst dancing on the jetty; share a bottle in a rowing boat as you watch jumping fish or whilst picnicking under a silvery moon; savour the spicy, buttery flavours of this unfiltered, coppery liquid infused with bog myrtle, yarrow, and juniper, and marvel that this age-old, oily composition remains wholly unchanged by time. Brewed in open wooden vats using a fermented mash of rye and barley, the sahti recipe has been transmitted through the generations by oral folklore to produce an annual yield for summer festivities. A measure of the importance of this primitive beer is that a 19th-century Finnish history book contains 400 stanzas about sahti brewing compared to just 200 about the creation of the world.

Shared toasts of *kippis* ('cheers') ring out across Finland's picturesque Lake Päijänne in summer when dozens of wooden cabins are used for romantic soirées and wedding parties. Finland's second largest watery expanse shimmers amidst blonde river reeds and forested islands as the sound of a tolling bell from a passing steam-hauled vessel signifies another sun-drenched engagement onboard. Family-owned paddleboats have plied Lake Paijanne's tranquil waters for over a century and are synonymous with summertime joy in the hearts and minds of every Finn. Finland has enough lakes and islands for every Finnish family to own one, yet on a journey along the 199 km (123 miles) of rocky shores and beach-strewn flanks of the Lake Paijanne, the only thing that matters is that this gift of space and nature is yours – for now.